# The National Destiny: Ofiyok!

By

Gumaa Lodongi

Copyright © 2024
All Rights Reserved

# Table of Contents

Dedication and Acknowledgments ....................................... i
About the Author ................................................. iv
Introduction ..................................................... 1
Chapter 1: Democracy ............................................. 7
Chapter 2: Governance ........................................... 17
Chapter 3: Education ............................................ 30
Chapter 4: Economy – Prosperity Rising .......................... 47
Chapter 5: Environment .......................................... 70
Chapter 6: Leadership ........................................... 85
Chapter 7: Policy .............................................. 100
Chapter 8: Female Empowerment .................................. 116
Chapter 9: Youth ............................................... 128
Chapter 10: Healthcare ......................................... 144
Chapter 11: Infrastructure ..................................... 160
Chapter 12: Military ........................................... 179
Chapter 13: Law & Order ........................................ 196
Chapter 14: Communism vs. Capitalism in the Sudanese Context ... 212
Chapter 15: Idealisms of Tribalism ............................. 225
Chapter 16: Language ........................................... 242
Conclusion ..................................................... 260

# Dedication and Acknowledgments

In "The National Destiny: Ofiyok," I am deeply humbled and honored to present this work, fueled by the profound progression found within my dreams and visions. From the very moment of my birth to the present, I have been captivated by the ideals and aspirations that have driven me to exemplify the highest standards and the pinnacle of Sudan's essence as one unified nation, Ofiyok. This book is a testament to Sudan's indomitable spirit, which has triumphed over countless trials and tribulations, and it is my fervent hope that it will endure the test of time.

First and foremost, I express my heartfelt gratitude to my beloved family: my father, Francis Loboy Ohiri, my mother, Asonta Odowa Ogeri, my grandparents Odowa and Odongi, and my grandmothers Ebatta and Ekoka. Your unconditional love, wisdom, and unwavering support have been the bedrock of my strength and resilience.

To my mentor, Ted Jaleta, and my former teachers—Lisa Poirier, Mrs. Gavin, Mr. Stawarze, Louise Kenyon, Mr. Majewski, Mrs. Schamerze, Mrs. Leboldus—thank you for guiding me on my educational journey and for instilling in me the passion for knowledge and growth.

I am indebted to my coaches, Dr. Robert Hall, Coach Pine, Coach Wade Bartlett, Coach Ottenbreitt, Coach Kot, and Coach Von, for their invaluable mentorship and unwavering belief in my potential, which has propelled me to achieve my best.

I extend my deepest appreciation to my dear friend and mentor, Babba Victor Odreha, James Otawari, Criss Angel, and the remarkable individuals who have inspired and influenced me, including Barack Obama, David Copperfield, David Blaine, Emma Watson, Oprah Winfrey, J.K. Rowling, Bill Gates, Will Smith, Angelina Jolie, Gayle King, Don Lemon, Brooke Baldwin, Mr. Bercianni, the University of Regina, Kosti Sudan, and Regina Saskatchewan, Canada. Your contributions have left an indelible mark on my personal and creative journey.

My gratitude extends to my uncles: Secondo, George, George Ohia, Osebit, Kasio, Maurice, Ben Oduho, and Steve Paterno, whose unwavering support and guidance have enriched my understanding of Sudan's diverse tapestry.

I also want to acknowledge the rich cultural heritage of the Latuka chiefs and every tribe in Sudan, whose enduring spirit has shaped my perspective and appreciation for our nation's unity.

To Africa and the global community, I extend my thanks for the vast array of influences that have broadened my horizons and deepened my understanding of the world.

Finally, I apologize if I inadvertently omitted anyone's name. Please know that each of you holds a special place in my heart, and your support resonates deeply within me. May God bless all my faithful admirers.

Once again, I express my heartfelt appreciation and dedicate this work to all those who have touched my life and contributed to my growth as an individual. Your love, guidance, and support have been instrumental in shaping my journey and the creation of "The National Destiny: Ofiyok."

# About the Author

Gumaa Francis Lodongi is a Sudanese-born author and entertainer who moved to Canada in search of better opportunities. With a passion for acting, modeling, inventing, entrepreneurship, humanitarianism, and politics, Gumaa aims to break down barriers and enliven humanity. Drawing inspiration from historical renaissance figures such as Leonardo da Vinci and David Michelangelo, he aspires to achieve similar levels of success and prosperity, but with his own unique twist.

Having spent the first nine years of his life in Sudan and the following 18 years in Canada, Gumaa has experienced a range of cultural assimilations. He wishes to use his personal experiences to enrich Canadian diversity and inspire hope, faith, and optimism in humanity. Through his book, he hopes to redefine the purpose of immigration, inhumanity, discrimination, and stereotypes, and to encourage individualistic inner and outer peace, regardless of one's racial, national, or religious background.

Gumaa is dedicated to the evolution of humanity and believes in the redemptive power of living an extraordinary life. He encourages his readers and listeners to maintain faith and offers insightful perspectives on his blogs and podcasts, The Circle of Life https://oceansofblues.blogspot.com/ , Ancestral Motivation https://anchor.fm/gumaa-francis-lodongi , The Peak of Passion https://anchor.fm/gumaa-lodongi , and #Humanity! https://anchor.fm/gumaa-lodongi5

# Introduction

Ever since I was a boy, I grew up with dreams far greater than the mirage that is seen in the Sahara desert – which is the peak of glory defining the potential for South Sudan and Sudan.

Despite the apparent intensity of the tensions, I had hoped for a swift resolution, allowing my beloved Nation to regain its freedom and thrive once more. I believe that as a result of the turmoil and hardships we endured before and during the war, we will attain a state of blissful joy. In this state, our children will be able to live freely, experiencing restoration and appreciation for life that surpasses the way our previous generations lived.

I believe joy will consume our hearts and drain away the tears from our eyes so that we can see clearly into the mirage of what the peak of the glory entails for our humanity. Joy is like a double edge sword; it knows joy, and it also knows conflict. It defends us at times of vulnerability, and it defeats us at times of vulnerability. Joy is a gift that I believe was given to humanity so that we may share with each other the gift of giving and celebrate those moments we affirm that we are one. I understand, very strongly, that joy is responsible for the love that we have for our nation and our land as long as we allow the relationships of our beings to flow like nature's scents making their way into the soil to reinforce the roots of a united nation.

Peace is what I like to believe is the underlying source for which resolution is sought after but not always the answer to the tensions we face as a nation. If you seek only love, then you will come to realize there is no need for peace because the path to peace is a never-ending struggle, and choosing to be in harmony is to love. I know full well when we always pursue peace, we are acknowledging the present time negatively rather than positively, and we stall ourselves in time, hence, the reference stalemate. We are stalling ourselves when we talk about peace rather than discussing peace from a perspective of problem-solution, and that is what causes humanity to suffer.

Suffering at the moment while trying to make it unfold won't work; instead, realizing the truth is that we live in a world of duality; where there is peace, there has to be conflict, and where there is conflict, there has to be peace. So, therefore, once we develop a new tactic to surmount issues, it becomes a newer tactic to deal with either a similar or different issue. I believe, though, we can live with hope for a better future filled with plenty of opportunities for humanity to make progress. Now that hope isn't short-term nor long-term, but its shelf life is dependent upon humanity's capability to reach for the stars with iron-clad perseverance and strong-willed determination.

As for our freedom, I believe we are granted in every possible way by our Almighty Creator unalienable rights and privileges that we must safeguard and maintain, for they are of great value to us and to our lineal descendants. Our freedom will be like the siren in the wilderness capturing the hearts of humanity. I believe freedom will come to the people of Sudan just like the land of cush and milk and honey finding its way to the promised land. I know surely well that people that are oppressed will be set free, and the ones that are discriminated against will be liberated. I know in my heart in times like these, justice will be served and will continue to be served to separate the wheat from the chaff, truth from lies, light from dark, and open up the doors so that Humanity may succeed. We will define ourselves as Sudanese, and in that independence, that isn't something illusory or elusive.

However, rather it is like the staff permanently penetrated into the deep earth that we call our land, representing those cherished national values that we hold so dear and bind us. Our independence will always be impenetrable; thus, we must be steadfast to the waving flag. It can never be taken from us by any foreigners, nor has it ever been taken from us because there is an inherent strand stronger than any predetermined division. Let us love our Humanity and our Nation and our land, for there is a lot to learn from and glean that is spiritual and materialistic resources.

I believe our faith is greater in our almighty creator because, as small or big as it is, we can enliven matter, change the infrastructure, brighten the future, embolden our youth, and uplift our elders. We must hold firm to our relationship with our almighty creator so that we can recognize the brotherhood and sisterhood in all of us. If we focus on what matters, that is finally faith, then we won't be so heavy-laden because we will increase in development and be free of worry and trouble. I believe harmony is one of the major keys to development because when we focus on our cultural differences and share our unique intelligence and also as a consequence, we recognize the common and interesting attributes we harmonize and create a wonderful centerpiece that is what we call the circle of life.

Let us congregate not just at geographical locations but also in our hearts and minds and enable our spirits to be the mechanism that drives mutual agreements and Humanity forward. I believe Sudan is very internally and externally rich but also latently rich. Our potential is massive, our culture is impactful, our land is extensive, our people are smart and educated, and our natural environment is full of extraordinary wildlife. We can be more successful. We can be more powerful, we must be wiser, we must be more disciplined, we will be more fulfilled, and we will be more prosperous against all odds.

I believe in these hopes and dreams that it isn't only mine but ours for our Sudanese Humanity and land. I believe if we focus on our dreams, focus on our efforts and willpower, focus on our locomotive force, focus on our vision. Our individual and collective dreams shall certainly come true. We must never give up, and we must never quit. We must always work hard and apply ourselves. For many of the great wonders in the globe weren't created in one day but several days. Therefore one, two, three, or four attempts don't make us failures but a successful history in the making.

I understand for a Nation to be united and cohesive, we should be living according to Humanitarianism and abiding by the golden rule. Living life without a sense of consideration for your fellow Humanity is disrespectful and inexcusable. We live in a day and age where opportunities are abundant, and we can employ them to support the foundation of our society. I believe love is the greatest source of all that not only unites differences but blends similarities and creates the sameness of opinions and ways to lead one's life. Love for each other irrespective of the difference in race and gender bridges the gap for there to be biodiversity. Love for our history binds the fabric of our society. Love for our Almighty Creator ensures us of the divine destiny that we are leading towards. I believe God will open the doors of our hearts and minds so we can pursue and achieve a world-class education.

Our sophistication and brilliance will shine to the entire universe of how great and capable we are. Our talent and skills in academics will be extraordinary. I have faith in these aspirations that not only I care so deeply about but we as an entire Humanity cares about. Oh, the people that are so disease-stricken and physically disabled, you will all be blessed and healed of your troubles and worries. As for women, your time is near when you will be in power and authority, for you all deserve to reap what you have sown, that is, the tireless efforts you employed to nurture your men and children. I am proud of you and what you have accomplished thus far in all areas of discipline. You are beautiful and educated but also strong and passionate.

I know very well against all odds you will be the dictator of your own life and lead Humanity because of your powerful and impactful emotional influence. I love you, Sudan. May God bless the entire globe, and may God bless Sudan (United)!

Anything is possible!

# Humanity!

I understand, very strongly, that joy is responsible for the love that we have for our Nation and our land as long as we allow the relationships of our beings to flow like nature's scents making their way into the soil to reinforce the roots of a united nation.

Gumaa Francis Lodongi

# Chapter 1: Democracy

When we look at a nation like Sudan, the first issue is democracy which causes there to be a question of who we are as a nation. Where are we right now in terms of present progress? And where are we leading in terms of evolutionary progress? I think for as far as Sudan has suffered for at least more than six decades of the civil war causes us

To be in shock and, at the same, in awe not just of the horrendous warring tensions that we possibly have faced but in awe of the transforming factor it ensues. As a Sudanese/Canadian author, I have always been dealing with the same perplexion that, as a nation, this long-term war that my country has faced is what allows me to be hopeful and optimistic for the future. And as far as I am concerned, I would like to unveil my thoughts in this book about the bright future Sudan is capable of having, that is, to be united in Peace, joy, and love. Just as the saying always goes, united, we stand, divided, we fall.

My mission is to bring about change for the Sudanese nation so that greatness may prevail through the democratic influence that the government should uphold as a responsibility for the nation to have justice, prosperity, and liberty.

In this chapter, I want to talk to you about democracy and what it means for us. Democracy, as defined, is a vote for the people by the people. Therefore the government must see its future through democratic means. In order to keep progress moving forward, the government should most certainly give opportunities there to contribute to the circle of life. That is, through elections, as it should happen, voting must be possible for the entire nation. I understand for the longest time on earth, with respect to some specific nations, there has been and always still be a political struggle between the government and Humanity.

When focusing on Sudan, there is a history of political uprisings by the scolding of the protesters towards the national government before the nation had divided physically and until now when both halves of the nation have become independent. It is still very much evident that the democracy that is promised and declared in the constitution is still questioned because of the government's failure to deliver on its promise to the nation. What becomes of our hope now as a nation if we so want to unite in peace, joy, and love?

Government officials must rally with each other to instill in us hope and faith in the possibilities of how democracy can shape us and mold us for the betterment of a nation. Hence as a consequence, we should, as I have always dreamt for our beloved nation to see through the dulled visibility that change must come through necessary elections that aren't rigged but permits there to be a possibility of how much involvement should the Humanity of the nations be. Because as I know very well that politics is like a coin, it is never one-sided but two-sided. On each side, there is the government, and there is the Humanity. Since democracy is government for Humanity by Humanity. What that really means is the government can never work alone because it is a public service, first and foremost, which is a service unto Humanity, and if it is so, Humanity is the recipient and is the reciprocation unto the government.

What that indicates is politics is a tug of war between them that not only causes friction, but it is the static electricity that attracts the beacon of Christ to shine and pave the way forward for the Humanity of Sudan to live in prosperity, justice, and liberty. Of course, the Divine Office is always in control and guiding the government toward reconciliation with Humanity as we develop this nation together.

We, as Humanity, have to answer to the government, and the government has to answer to the divine office. The ability we have to answer to the government is not by how obedient we are towards them but by how we can also voice our concerns and speak about the underlying tensions we have in our hearts as we try to live a peaceful life of solidarity and strength. That is why I like to say that instead of opposing each other and making this a constant battle between us. We should, we must, we can, and we will work hand in hand because it takes two to tango.

The disfavors of democracy begin with the inability of a nation to be rooted in inclusivity because of the failures of the government to underscore tasks with the hierarchical powers in charge. I state this because, in a democracy, all are involved in the elective decisions to support those candidates in order to elect those authorities to put them in office so that they can control and govern the nation with the agenda of its national citizens in mind. I also think it's nearly impossible for the government to thrive when democracy puts those people that are overage in favor of the people that are underage. Because it causes for there to be cynicism in voting due to the demographic imbalance. It is unbeneficial for the government and Humanity to share the circle of life in democracy when one side of the coin is greater than the other in the sense that the elections can be rigged when elections are handled in a way that is careless and favoring a despotic party over the interests of the innocent lives of its national citizens.

I also would like to think democracy can be a weak form of government when the politicians or statesmen choose to serve their own agenda under the guise of a power struggle that can tear away at the pure gullibility of the nation's citizens who don't know any better however to follow in the trails of their leaders as like the blind leading the blind. The efficiency of the government is in lack thereof because of the mishandling and abuse of democracy in the interests of

South Sudan and Sudan. These types of inefficiencies of our government in South Sudan and Sudan are slowly degrading the values and principles of our Nation as a whole since the beginning of the strike of civil wars until the day when we gained our independence to the juncture in which we are now becoming inclined to be more aware and heartily ingrained deeply into the roots of what makes us South Sudanese and Sudanese; our pride mainly.

The values and principles I like to believe that I see in my vision for what we always latently have been and are going to be as who we are as one people, one nation justified and founded in justice, prosperity, and liberty. To put it simply, that is what ought to drive our democracy, that is, justice, prosperity, and liberty, and not the nonsense of who ought to be served first, that is, either me, or him, or even her. Or the arguments we have with each other stating inhumanity things to each other that indicate openly and hurtfully how much we disrespect, dislike, and even loathe those people that worship differently higher powers that we may not worship, look different than we do, behave strangely or even overall lead not similar or different lives than how we are living. Because when we look at politics from this viewpoint, the agendas of our statesmen and politicians are served at the risk of Humanity, who are us, the South Sudanese and Sudanese.

What are the problems that we need to troubleshoot lies not at the core of the lack of good democracy or, as I said previously, misused or mismanaged democracy; however, the problems are embedded deeply in the land itself, causing the country to stagger in independence, freedom, peace, justice, prosperity, and liberty. How we can come to resolve these issues by looking at the true essence of democracy really and not undervaluing it but serving its interests of it. Because even though they say democracy is for the people by the people, I like to maintain that democracy is actually Humanity is driven because it irrigates the decisions from the source of the ruling authorities, such as the President, vice president, and cabinet, all the way to the members of the legislative body.

Democracy, that is without bias or discrimination, is the democracy that we can count on that can lead us and empower us like the waters of the Nile dam inciting electricity that makes the decisions of the ruling body in the government have a say with meaning and intent. Democracy that is without injustice or racism is the kind that we don't want because the opposite is all good and all-wise, keeping our land free of debris and corruption, our people infused in togetherness and belongingness, and the floods of our bloodshed pumping our hearts to have kindness and be loving Humanity to our next door neighbors giving them a second chance of redemption because that is what recycles the alpha and omega of our relationships, whether that is in business, government, or even national and foreign affairs. Regarding the antithesis of the disadvantages of democracy, there lies the basis of beneficial favors of democracy that affects the political engagement within its own chamber of legislators and draws in the focus of the citizens prompting an about way of rejuvenating the nations. If you're confusing this with civic engagement, well, you're wrong because, as far as I know, the powers of politics are a democracy but not limited to; instead, it is also theocracy, democracy, and libertarianism in sequence. The power is not just in how democracy affects civilians but in how civilians affect political leaders allowing there to be a circle of life. Theocracy is of key importance in who we worship. Democracy is of vital importance in how we treat each other with respect to power that comes from giving citizens their just or fair voting rights. Libertarianism is of true importance in how we can rid ourselves as Humanity, that is, either the civilians or politicians of disagreeable hypocrisy that tears the fabric of our waving the national flag.

Another component of democracy being advantageous when used in the right and proper manner is it actually paints a picture of our true ideals as a nation or as when an artist like David Michelangelo painted the Sistine Chapel. The government is David Michelangelo, the people are the Sistine Chapel, and the overall foundation is the land which we live on with our Sudanese (Ofiyok) flag waving with pride that is like a double edge sword. It defends us in times of vulnerability and is the diplomacy that with we live by, the true integrity of our relationships with our fellow neighbors and the neighboring countries surrounding us around the entire planet Earth. I have a vision, and it is my mission to change, shape, and mold Sudan which will be called Ofiyok at the advent of peace, solidarity, freedom, independence, justice, prosperity, and liberty. A time where there will be no more war, a time where no more hardship or strife, a time where there will be no more pain or anguish. I have a vision for Ofiyok that it will most surely be called a land of milk and honey, a land of cush, a land of utopian liberty.

I have a dream that one day, my people will be set free from the history of colonization and invasion that lingers like a wound that doesn't let up. I have a dream that in this day and age, with the introduction of technology, education will be vast and evermore present so that we can learn and grow boundlessly. I have high hopes and aspirations that are shared collectively with the oneness of the past, present, and future, which we rely on the most.

Well, I like to state that although Sudan is now the Past, Ofiyok is the reemergence of the possibilities we share as one people and one united nation. Lord, I believe that today is the day when drudgery will be no more, slavery will be no more, persecution will be no more, oppression will be no more, and Inhumanity will be no more. Although Sudan is of the past, Ofiyok will be a land with Nile rivers, oceans flowing through, acacia trees, Nubian mountains, among mountains, Nubian desert, Sahara desert, etc, making the connections that last for eternity in our minds of the true Sistine chapel that our future theocratic, democratic, and libertarian government is made of. A new day and a new horizon are the essences of the peace we will particularly have.

My hope is unending, and your hopes should be everlasting because it takes two to tango. Oh lord, let peace come to the land of Ofiyok and let paradise land atop the pillars of loyalty, commitment, discipline, divinity, devotion, and honor, that we may glorify and praise Ofiyok, the land that is home to us, the Nilotics, Arabs, Caucasians, Asians, Latin Americans and entirely anybody who will be seeking asylum or refuge in the land of cush and milk and honey. Ofiyok will always be open to welcoming immigrants from anywhere across the globe for the betterment of their residence and feel comfortable calling Ofiyok a home.

Going back to talk about democracy again, it is an assurance in its utmost respect that the very own definition of democracy is important in its essence to duplicate the powers of the government unto the people by means of tactful and diplomatic relationships between the electorate and the electors. This importance can't be dismissed because it provides remarkable evidence of the potential democracy has of effectuality to the Humanity of Ofiyok. Why is democracy important? Because it opens doorways of opportunities for there to be a replacement of those people in governmental offices because, in that aspect, change can always be inevitable, and authoritarianism can never be tolerated. Democracy is far greater than authoritarianism because the powers of voting are in the hands of the nation's citizens, and they get to make a choice for who should lead them. And this is, without a doubt, an unveiling truth because it is the certainty that everybody else in the nation, that is, the Humanity citizens, can depend on.

# Chapter 2: Governance

In a world where the winds of change constantly sweep across nations, there exists a place of great promise and untapped potential: Sudan. As I stand on the precipice of this remarkable country's transformation, I am filled with an unwavering sense of hope and enthusiasm. The topic that stirs my soul and ignites my passion is none other than governance – the very foundation upon which a prosperous and united Sudan shall be built.

Governance, the art and science of effective leadership, holds within it the power to shape the destiny of nations. It is a vibrant tapestry of principles, values, and institutions that can guide a society towards progress, unity, and justice. It is the fulcrum upon which the dreams and aspirations of a nation rest, and it is with great fervor that I embark on this exploration of governance in the context of Sudan.

Sudan, a land brimming with history, diversity, and resilience, has weathered storms of uncertainty and upheaval. Yet, from the depths of struggle, a resounding spirit of resilience has emerged, beckoning us towards a brighter future. It is within this spirit that I find my purpose – to envision a Sudan where governance becomes a beacon of light, illuminating the path towards unity, prosperity, and equitable development.

As I delve into the intricacies of governance in Sudan, I invite you, dear readers, to join me on this journey of exploration. Together, let us embrace the challenges, seek the opportunities, and forge a collective vision for a Sudan that stands tall among nations. Through an interactive dialogue, I aim to share my dreams, aspirations, and ideals for the governance of this remarkable country, and in doing so, inspire you to join hands in shaping the future of Sudan.

With every word written and every idea expressed, I hope to kindle a spark within your hearts, igniting a flame of optimism and belief in the transformative power of effective governance. For it is through the collaboration of passionate individuals like yourselves that Sudan will rise, reunited, and bask in the glory of its dreams and visions.

Together, let us embark on this intellectual journey, exploring the multifaceted dimensions of governance and envisioning a Sudan that shines as a beacon of progress, prosperity, and unity. The time is now to unravel the tapestry of governance and together weave a future that surpasses all expectations.

Join me, as we set forth on this remarkable odyssey of hope, as we uncover the keys to unlocking Sudan's boundless potential. The voyage begins, and the possibilities are infinite.

Throughout my life's journey, I have witnessed firsthand the profound impact that governance can have on the destiny of a nation. Growing up in Sudan, I experienced the ebb and flow of governance systems, from times of uncertainty and turmoil to moments of hope and progress. These experiences have left an indelible mark on my perception of the world and have shaped my deep-rooted belief in the transformative power of effective governance.

I recall vividly the days when governance in Sudan seemed marred by inefficiency, corruption, and a lack of transparency. The consequences of such governance were palpable in the lives of ordinary citizens. Basic services were scarce, opportunities were limited, and the trust between the people and their leaders eroded. It was during these challenging times that I yearned for change, for a governance system that would prioritize the needs and aspirations of the Sudanese people.

However, amid the struggles, I also witnessed glimpses of what effective governance can achieve. I saw the positive impact of inclusive policies that brought communities together, fostering a sense of unity and shared purpose. I observed dedicated individuals who selflessly served their fellow citizens, striving to create a better future for all. These experiences served as a beacon of hope, reminding me of the immense potential that lies within the realm of governance.

Effective governance is not merely a bureaucratic concept; it is the lifeblood that courses through the veins of a nation, fueling its progress and fostering an environment of prosperity and social harmony. It is through effective governance that a nation can achieve sustainable development, ensuring the equitable distribution of resources, opportunities, and justice.

When governance is strong, transparent, and accountable, it becomes a catalyst for social and economic advancement. It provides a solid foundation upon which individuals can thrive, fostering an environment conducive to entrepreneurship, innovation, and the unleashing of human potential. Effective governance empowers citizens, giving them a voice in decision-making processes and creating avenues for their active participation in shaping the future of their nation.

Conversely, the absence or inadequacy of effective governance can lead to stagnation, inequality, and social unrest. It hampers the realization of a nation's true potential and denies its citizens the opportunities they deserve. It is therefore imperative that we recognize the pivotal role governance plays in the progress of Sudan and the well-being of its people.

As we explore the possibilities and envision the future of governance in Sudan, let us bear in mind the transformative power it holds. Together, we can strive for a governance system that not only addresses the challenges of today but also lays a solid groundwork for the dreams and visions we hold for the future. Let us embrace the principles of transparency, accountability, and inclusivity, for they are the cornerstones upon which effective governance is built.

Through our collective efforts and unwavering commitment to good governance, we can usher in an era of progress, unity, and prosperity for Sudan. It is with this conviction that I embark on this journey, eager to share my dreams and ideals for the governance of Sudan and to inspire others to join me in shaping a future where effective governance reigns supreme.

Together, let us forge a path towards a Sudan that stands tall among nations, driven by a governance system that reflects the aspirations and values of its people.

The current state of governance in Sudan is a reflection of the complex challenges that the nation has faced over the years. It is a tapestry woven with both triumphs and setbacks, progress and obstacles. While strides have been made towards democratic reforms and transitional governance, there is still much work to be done to establish a robust and inclusive system that serves the interests of all Sudanese citizens.

Sudan stands at a pivotal moment in its history, as it strives to build a governance framework that upholds the principles of justice, equality, and the rule of law. It is essential to acknowledge the existing gaps and deficiencies in governance, which have hindered the full realization of the nation's potential. These challenges include corruption, lack of accountability, and a need for greater transparency in decision-making processes.

Amidst the current challenges, I am filled with unwavering optimism for the future of governance in Sudan. I firmly believe that the nation has the capacity to overcome the hurdles and embark on a transformative journey towards a brighter and more prosperous future. The winds of change are blowing, and the aspirations of the Sudanese people are calling for a governance system that empowers, uplifts, and ensures the well-being of all.

Sudan possesses immense potential, both in its human capital and its rich resources. It is a nation brimming with talent, resilience, and a deep longing for progress. With concerted efforts, dedication, and a shared vision, we can harness this potential and steer Sudan towards a new era of governance that reflects the dreams and aspirations of its people.

To realize our vision for governance in Sudan, it is imperative to embrace a set of guiding principles and values that lay the foundation for a just and inclusive society. These principles should include:

**Transparency and Accountability**: Upholding transparency in decision-making processes, ensuring that the actions of public officials are subject to scrutiny, and establishing robust mechanisms for accountability are crucial for building trust between the government and its citizens.

**Rule of Law**: A strong commitment to the rule of law is essential for fostering a just and equitable society. This involves ensuring equal access to justice, promoting human rights, and safeguarding the rights and freedoms of all individuals.

**Participation and Inclusivity**: Governance in Sudan should be built upon the active participation of all citizens, irrespective of gender, ethnicity, or social background. Inclusivity entails creating spaces for dialogue, engaging diverse voices, and ensuring that marginalized communities have a seat at the table.

**Economic Development and Social Justice**: An effective governance system should prioritize economic development that is sustainable, inclusive, and benefits all segments of society. It should address poverty, reduce inequalities, and provide opportunities for employment and entrepreneurship.

**National Unity and Reconciliation**: Promoting national unity, fostering reconciliation, and healing the wounds of the past are essential for building a cohesive and harmonious society. It requires acknowledging the diversity of Sudan and celebrating its cultural heritage while striving for a shared sense of national identity.

By embracing these principles and values, Sudan can pave the way for a governance system that empowers its citizens, promotes social justice, and unlocks the nation's true potential.

Furthermore, transforming governance in Sudan requires a comprehensive and holistic approach that addresses the systemic challenges and promotes positive change. It necessitates a departure from old practices and the adoption of new strategies that align with the aspirations of the Sudanese people. Key transformations include:

**Institutional Strengthening**: Building strong and resilient institutions is vital for effective governance. This involves enhancing their capacity, promoting professionalism, and ensuring independence from undue influence. Strengthening institutions will foster a culture of good governance that is built on integrity, competence, and accountability.

**Decentralization and Local Governance:** Empowering local communities and decentralizing decision-making processes can lead to more responsive and inclusive governance. By devolving power to local levels, citizens can actively participate in shaping policies and programs that directly affect their lives. Local governance structures should be established to ensure that communities have a voice in decision-making and the allocation of resources.

According to me, transparency, accountability, and citizen participation are the cornerstones of good governance. They create an environment of trust, foster effective decision-making, and ensure that the needs and aspirations of the Sudanese people are at the forefront. It is essential to:

**Enhance Transparency**: Transparency in governance processes, such as budget allocations, public procurement, and decision-making, is crucial. By providing access to information, Sudanese citizens can hold their leaders accountable and actively participate in public affairs. This can be achieved through the implementation of robust transparency mechanisms and the promotion of open data initiatives.

**Strengthen Accountability Mechanisms**:

Accountability mechanisms must be established to ensure that public officials are answerable for their actions. This involves creating independent oversight bodies, encouraging whistleblowing protection, and enforcing the rule of law. By holding individuals accountable for their conduct, Sudan can prevent corruption, promote integrity, and build public trust.

**Foster Citizen Participation**: Engaging citizens in decision-making processes is essential for inclusive governance. This can be done through public consultations, participatory budgeting, and citizen feedback mechanisms. By actively involving citizens, their perspectives and expertise can inform policies and initiatives, resulting in more effective and people-centered governance.

I believe that several initiatives and reforms can contribute to better governance in Sudan. These include:

**Strengthening Anti-Corruption Measures**:

Implementing robust anti-corruption strategies, establishing specialized anti-corruption commissions, and promoting a culture of integrity are essential. This includes enforcing anti-corruption laws, enhancing financial transparency, and conducting thorough investigations into corruption allegations.

**Building a Digital Government**: Embracing digital technologies can streamline administrative processes, improve service delivery, and enhance citizen-government interaction. Initiatives such as e-governance, digital platforms for public services, and online citizen engagement can increase efficiency, transparency, and accessibility.

**Promoting Civil Society Engagement**: Recognizing and supporting the role of civil society organizations is crucial for promoting good governance. Encouraging their participation in policy formulation, monitoring government performance, and advocating for citizens' rights strengthens democratic processes and accountability.

**Strengthening Judicial Independence**: Ensuring the independence of the judiciary is paramount for upholding the rule of law. Reforms that enhance judicial independence, improve the efficiency of courts, and provide adequate resources for the administration of justice can bolster public trust in the legal system.

**Investing in Public Service Excellence**: Attracting, training, and retaining competent public servants is vital for effective governance. Investing in human resource development, merit-based recruitment, and performance evaluation systems can enhance the professionalism and efficiency of the public sector.

By implementing these initiatives and embracing transformative reforms, Sudan can pave the way for a governance system.

Unity and reconciliation are pivotal for Sudan's progress and stability. The wounds of the past need to heal, and divisions must be bridged to forge a united nation. It is essential to acknowledge the challenges and grievances that have plagued Sudanese society, and actively work towards healing and reconciliation.

Inclusive governance plays a vital role in fostering national unity. By ensuring that all voices are heard, regardless of ethnicity, religion, or region, Sudan can build a sense of belonging and shared destiny among its diverse population. Inclusive governance encourages dialogue, promotes understanding, and embraces the richness of Sudan's cultural mosaic.

Through inclusive governance, Sudan can provide equal opportunities for participation, representation, and resource allocation. It involves actively engaging marginalized communities, empowering women and youth, and promoting social cohesion. By recognizing and respecting the rights of all Sudanese citizens, inclusive governance strengthens the bonds that hold the nation together.

Throughout Sudan's history, there have been remarkable instances where unity and reconciliation have triumphed over division and conflict. Stories of communities coming together, overcoming differences, and rebuilding their lives illustrate the power of unity.

For instance, in the aftermath of conflicts, grassroots movements have emerged, advocating for peace, justice, and reconciliation. These movements bring together individuals from different backgrounds who are united by a shared vision for a better Sudan. They serve as beacons of hope, inspiring others to embrace unity and work towards a brighter future.

Personal anecdotes of individuals who have experienced the transformative power of reconciliation can also highlight the importance of forgiveness and understanding. These stories showcase how the healing of personal and communal wounds can pave the way for a united and prosperous Sudan.

Finally, we should know that the significance of governance in Sudan's journey towards progress and prosperity. The vision for Sudan's governance is rooted in unity, inclusivity, and the pursuit of national reconciliation.

Our vision for Sudan's governance is one of transparency, integrity, and responsiveness. We dream of a Sudan where all citizens are empowered, where institutions are strong and accountable, and where unity and reconciliation prevail. We envision a nation where diversity is celebrated, and every Sudanese has an equal opportunity to thrive and contribute to the nation's development.

As we conclude this chapter, let us remember that the dreams and visions for Sudan's governance are not distant aspirations but achievable realities. It is a collective responsibility to contribute to the transformation of governance in Sudan. Each one of us has a role to play, whether through active citizen engagement, supporting reforms, or advocating for unity and reconciliation.

Let us stand together, Sudanese brothers and sisters, united in our quest for a brighter future. With perseverance, determination, and a shared commitment to good governance, we can create the Sudan we envision—one that upholds the values of justice, equality, and opportunity for all.

Together, let us embrace the journey towards a Sudan where governance truly serves the dreams and aspirations of its people. The path may be challenging, but our unity, resilience, and unwavering hope will guide us towards a brighter tomorrow.

## Chapter 3: Education

Education possesses an unparalleled transformative potential that can shape individuals and societies alike. Its influence extends far beyond classrooms, textbooks, and exams. Education acts as a catalyst for personal growth, empowering individuals to reach their fullest potential while also serving as a driver of societal progress.

As I embark on this journey through the realms of education in the nation of Sudan, my heart brims with optimism and idealism. In my vision for the future of South Sudan and Sudan, I see a united land where dreams are nurtured, potential is realized, and the ideals of education shape the destiny of its people. Imagine, if you will, a Sudan that rises from the very bottom to the pinnacle of the totem pole, surpassing the wonders and luxuries witnessed in the farthest corners of the globe.

Education, my dear readers, is the fulcrum upon which this transformation rests. It is the driving force that will catapult Sudan, or as I fondly call it, Ofiyok, into an era of unparalleled progress and prosperity. With unwavering idealism and boundless determination, we shall forge a path where education becomes the cornerstone of our society, igniting the flames of knowledge and empowering our people to become agents of change.

Picture a nation where every child, irrespective of their background or circumstance, has access to quality education.

It is a place where schools resonate with the joyful chatter of eager minds, where teachers stand as beacons of inspiration, and where students embrace learning as a lifelong adventure. In the classrooms of Ofiyok, knowledge will flow like a mighty river, nourishing the intellects of the young and fostering a hunger for discovery.

But education in Ofiyok goes beyond textbooks and academic rigors. It encompasses a holistic approach that nourishes the mind, body, and soul. We shall cultivate an environment where creativity flourishes, where critical thinking thrives, and where values of compassion, empathy, and respect for all humankind take root. In the embrace of such an education, our youth will emerge as well-rounded individuals, equipped not only with knowledge but also with the tools to navigate the complexities of the world.

In this idealistic vision, education becomes a force of transformation, extending its reach beyond classrooms and into the farthest corners of our nation. We shall invest in the training and professional development of our teachers, recognizing them as the torchbearers of knowledge, passion, and inspiration. Through their unwavering dedication, they shall shape the hearts and minds of future generations, nurturing the seeds of innovation, and awakening the inherent brilliance that resides within each child.

In Ofiyok, we shall transcend the boundaries of traditional education and embrace technological advancements as catalysts for progress. Our classrooms will be equipped with cutting-edge tools, opening doors to a world of limitless possibilities. We shall harness the power of digital platforms to connect students across the nation, fostering collaboration and cultural exchange, transcending physical limitations, and ushering in a new era of interconnected learning.

Ultimately, the vision is to develop an education system that nurtures well-rounded individuals, grounded in strong values and equipped with the knowledge and skills to contribute meaningfully to their communities and shape Sudan's future.

By embarking on this transformative journey, Sudan can unlock the full potential of its people and pave the way for a prosperous and inclusive society. Education will be the driving force behind this transformation, shaping not only individuals but also Sudan as a whole.

**Challenges and Opportunities in Sudan's Education System**

Despite the transformative power of education, Sudan faces various challenges in its education system. However, these challenges also present opportunities for innovation and reform. By addressing these obstacles head-on, Sudan can revolutionize its education system and create a brighter future for its citizens.

### A. Challenges in Sudan's Education System

**Limited Access to Education**: Geographical barriers and lack of infrastructure restrict access to education, particularly in rural and remote areas.

Socioeconomic disparities prevent marginalized communities from accessing quality education, perpetuating inequality.

Conflict and displacement disrupt educational opportunities, leaving many children and youth without access to schooling.

**Quality of Education:** Insufficient resources, outdated curricula, and inadequate teacher training contribute to a lack of quality education.

Limited access to technology and digital resources hinders students' ability to acquire 21st-century skills.

Disparities in educational standards across different regions and institutions further exacerbate the quality gap.

**Gender Disparities:** Deep-rooted cultural norms and practices continue to limit girls' access to education, particularly in rural areas.

Early marriage, gender-based violence, and societal expectations often result in lower enrollment and higher dropout rates among girls.

Addressing gender disparities in education is crucial for achieving gender equality and unlocking the full potential of Sudan's population.

### B. Opportunities for Reform and Innovation

**Embracing Technology:** Leveraging digital tools and online platforms can expand access to education, especially in underserved areas. Another vital fulcrum for a country like Sudan to evolve is to keenly observe and actively participate in the rapid advancement of technology. In doing so, we not only enable ourselves to strive for a higher and much superior understanding of education but also foster cultural growth, community engagement, national prosperity, internal independence, and position ourselves on the global platform of trade and diplomacy's most intricate and innovative chapters. Technology-enabled learning becomes a beacon not only to enhance educational experiences and promote interactive learning but also to bridge the digital divide that may hinder our progress on both national and global fronts.

**Teacher Training and Professional Development:** Investing in comprehensive teacher training programs can improve the quality of education across Sudan.

Professional development opportunities can equip teachers with innovative teaching methods and foster continuous learning.

**Curriculum Enhancement:** Updating curricula to align with the needs of the 21st century can prepare students for future challenges and opportunities.

Incorporating critical thinking, problem-solving, and creativity into the curriculum can foster a culture of innovation and adaptability.

**Community Engagement and Partnerships:** Collaborating with local communities, NGOs, and international organizations can enhance educational opportunities and bridge gaps in access and quality.

Engaging parents and community members in education decision-making can foster a sense of ownership and promote accountability.

**Empowering Girls and Women:** Implementing targeted initiatives to address gender disparities in education can ensure equal opportunities for girls and women.

Encouraging girls' enrollment, providing safe learning environments, and challenging societal norms can create a more inclusive education system.

By recognizing these challenges as opportunities for growth and implementing strategic reforms, Sudan can revolutionize its education system. With a commitment to inclusivity, quality, and innovation, Sudan can unlock the full potential of its citizens, nurturing a generation that will drive the nation's progress and prosperity.

Before delving into the vision for transforming education in Sudan, it is essential to recognize the urgent need for change. While Part II highlighted the existing challenges in Sudan's governance system, it is equally important to acknowledge the impact of these challenges on the education sector. The current state of education in Sudan reflects a system in need of revitalization and innovation. However, within these challenges lie immense opportunities to reshape the educational landscape and pave the way for a brighter future.

### A. Addressing the Gaps and Inequities

**Quality Disparities:** Disparities in the quality of education between urban and rural areas, as well as among different socioeconomic groups, have perpetuated inequalities.

Insufficient infrastructure, lack of qualified teachers, and inadequate learning resources have hindered educational opportunities for many Sudanese children.

**Gender Disparity:** Despite progress, gender disparities in education persist, particularly in access and retention rates for girls.

Empowering girls with education is not only a matter of equality but also a crucial step towards social and economic development.

**Skills Mismatch:** The misalignment between the skills acquired through formal education and the demands of the job market has created a mismatch that hinders economic growth.

Addressing this gap requires a focus on equipping students with relevant, practical skills and fostering entrepreneurship.

## B. Embracing the Transformative Power of Education

**Education as a Catalyst for Change:** Education has the power to transform individuals, communities, and nations.

By investing in education, Sudan can unlock the potential of its citizens, foster innovation, and drive sustainable development.

**Meeting the Challenges of the Future:** Rapid technological advancements, evolving job markets, and global interconnectedness necessitate an education system that prepares individuals for the challenges of the future.

Sudan must equip its youth with the skills, knowledge, and mindset to navigate an increasingly complex and interconnected world.

**Empowering the Youth:** The youth of Sudan represent a vast pool of talent and potential.

By providing them with quality education, opportunities for skill development, and platforms for engagement, Sudan can harness their energy and creativity to shape a brighter future.

By recognizing the need for educational transformation and understanding the challenges and opportunities that lie ahead, Sudan can embark on a journey towards a revitalized and progressive education system. The next section will explore the vision and strategies for transforming education in Sudan, ensuring that it becomes a pillar of national development and individual empowerment.

As Sudan envisions a future where education is at the forefront of its development, key strategies and initiatives can shape a transformative education system that empowers individuals, promotes societal progress, and drives economic growth. By embracing these transformative approaches, Sudan can lay the foundation for a brighter and more prosperous future.

### A. Holistic Approach to Education

**Integrated Curriculum:** Developing a curriculum that integrates academic knowledge, practical skills, and values cultivates well-rounded individuals.

Incorporating subjects such as entrepreneurship, financial literacy, and environmental sustainability equips students with the tools needed for success in the modern world.

**Focus on Critical Thinking and Problem-Solving:** Shifting the emphasis from rote memorization to critical thinking and problem-solving skills prepares students to navigate complex challenges.

Encouraging students to analyze, evaluate, and propose innovative solutions fosters a culture of creativity and entrepreneurship.

**Character Development:** Nurturing ethical values, empathy, and social responsibility alongside academic learning fosters responsible citizenship and promotes a harmonious society.

Encouraging community service, leadership development, and teamwork instills qualities that contribute to the holistic growth of students.

**B. Inclusive and Equitable Education**

**Universal Access***:* Ensuring that every child, regardless of their background, has equal access to quality education is paramount.

Removing barriers to education, including gender disparities, disability inclusivity, and socioeconomic inequalities, is crucial for an inclusive society.

**Early Childhood Education:** Investing in early childhood education programs prepares young learners for a successful educational journey.

Quality early childhood education fosters cognitive, emotional, and social development, laying a strong foundation for future learning.

**Lifelong Learning:** Promoting a culture of lifelong learning encourages individuals to pursue continuous education and adapt to evolving societal needs.

Providing adult education and vocational training opportunities equips individuals with the skills required for career advancement and personal growth.

### C. Innovation and Technology Integration

**Digital Transformation:** Embracing technology as an integral part of the education system enhances teaching and learning experiences.

Utilizing e-learning platforms, interactive digital resources, and educational apps expands access, engagement, and personalized learning opportunities.

**STEM Education:** Prioritizing science, technology, engineering, and mathematics (STEM) education prepares students for the demands of the future job market.

Encouraging hands-on learning, scientific inquiry, and problem-based projects fosters critical STEM skills and nurtures innovation.

**Teacher Empowerment:** Equipping teachers with digital skills and providing professional development opportunities in educational technology enhances their effectiveness in the digital age.

Creating supportive environments for teachers to experiment with innovative teaching methodologies fosters a culture of continuous improvement.

### D. Partnership and Collaboration

**Public-Private Partnerships:** Collaborating with private entities, NGOs, and civil society organizations can amplify the impact of educational initiatives.

Public-private partnerships bring together diverse resources, expertise, and networks to address education challenges collectively.

**International Cooperation:** Engaging with international organizations and leveraging global expertise can provide valuable insights and support for educational reforms.

Sharing best practices, participating in exchange programs, and accessing funding opportunities contribute to the advancement of Sudan's education system.

**Community Engagement:** Encouraging active involvement of parents, families, and community stakeholders in education decision-making ensures a shared responsibility for the success of students.

Establishing school management committees, parent-teacher associations, and community-driven initiatives fosters a sense of ownership and promotes accountability.

By adopting a holistic approach, prioritizing inclusivity, embracing innovation, and fostering collaboration, Sudan can transform its education system. With a shared vision and collective effort, Sudan can build a future where education serves as a catalyst for individual growth, societal development, and national prosperity.

## Empowering Sudanese Youth through Education and Innovation

By investing in quality education, enhancing infrastructure, and equipping teachers with the necessary tools, we lay the groundwork for a generation empowered with knowledge and skills. Simultaneously, we embrace the spirit of innovation, fostering an environment that nurtures creativity, collaboration, and entrepreneurial thinking. Through inclusive education practices, transformative curricula, and the cultivation of innovation hubs, we empower Sudanese youth to become architects of change and contributors to our nation's progress.

**A. Investing in Quality Education:**

**Enhancing Infrastructure**: Upgrading and expanding educational facilities to provide a conducive learning environment for all students.

Equipping schools with modern technology and resources to support effective teaching and learning.

**Strengthening Teacher Training:** Investing in comprehensive professional development programs to improve the quality and effectiveness of teaching.

Attracting and retaining qualified teachers through competitive salaries, incentives, and support systems.

**Curriculum Transformation**: Updating the curriculum to align with the needs of the 21st-century world.

Incorporating subjects that promote critical thinking, problem-solving, creativity, and digital literacy.

### B. Fostering Innovation and Entrepreneurship

**Creating Innovation Hubs:** Establishing innovation centers and hubs where students can explore their creativity, collaborate, and develop innovative solutions to local and global challenges.

Encouraging interdisciplinary projects that integrate science, technology, engineering, arts, and mathematics (STEAM) education.

**Encouraging Entrepreneurship:** Providing entrepreneurship education and mentorship programs to nurture entrepreneurial skills among students.

Facilitating access to funding, resources, and networks for aspiring young entrepreneurs to start their ventures.

**Collaboration with Industries:** Forging partnerships with industries to bridge the gap between education and the job market.

Offering internships, apprenticeships, and hands-on experiences that expose students to real-world challenges and foster employability skills.

## Education as a Catalyst for National Transformation

### A. Empowering the Youth as Agents of Change

As we strive to shape a brighter future, it is imperative to recognize the crucial role of the youth as catalysts for transformation. Education plays a pivotal role in empowering young minds with the knowledge, skills, and values needed to drive positive change. By fostering leadership skills and promoting civic engagement, we nurture a generation of active citizens who are capable of taking ownership of their communities and contributing to the nation's progress. Through educational programs that prioritize entrepreneurship and provide job opportunities, we equip young Sudanese individuals with the tools they need to become innovators, creators, and drivers of economic growth.

### B. Education as a Driver of Social Cohesion and Cultural Preservation

Education serves as a bridge that connects diverse communities, celebrating our rich tapestry of cultures and traditions while fostering social cohesion. By embracing and celebrating our collective diversity, we create an inclusive society where all individuals feel valued and respected. Through education, we instill in our youth a deep appreciation for their cultural heritage, preserving the traditions and customs that make Sudan unique. By creating opportunities for intercultural dialogue and understanding, we nurture a sense of unity that transcends differences and strengthens the fabric of our nation.

**C. The Long-term Impact of an Educated Society**

An educated society is the cornerstone of sustainable development and economic growth. By investing in education, we equip individuals with the skills and knowledge necessary to thrive in a rapidly evolving world. A well-educated workforce fuels innovation, drives productivity, and attracts investment, leading to economic prosperity. Moreover, education creates a ripple effect that extends beyond individual success, contributing to the overall advancement of society. As more Sudanese individuals access quality education, we lay the groundwork for a prosperous future, where every citizen can contribute to the nation's growth and well-being.

By empowering the youth as agents of change, fostering social cohesion, preserving our cultural heritage, and driving sustainable development, we pave the way for a prosperous and harmonious nation. As we continue to invest in education, we unlock the limitless potential of our people, securing a brighter future for Sudan and its citizens.

As we're moving towards the end of this chapter, dear readers, let us remember the profound words of Malcolm X.

*"Education is the passport to the future, for tomorrow belongs to those who prepare for it today."*

*- Malcolm X*

Education is indeed the key that unlocks the doors to a brighter future. It also serves as a driver of social cohesion, celebrating diversity and preserving our cultural heritage. Moreover, education contributes to sustainable development and economic growth, securing a prosperous future for Sudan. Our vision is to revolutionize the education system, making it accessible, inclusive, and of high quality. By embracing this vision, we inspire hope and motivation for the future, as we unite in our efforts to create a society where every individual can fulfill their potential. Together, we can build a nation where education becomes the catalyst for a brighter and more promising Sudan.

# Chapter 4: Economy – Prosperity Rising

Amidst the dawning of a new era for Sudan, where dreams and visions materialize, the resurgent nation stands poised to revolutionize its economic landscape. As we delve into the realm of prosperity and growth, illuminating the path that will elevate the economy of Sudan (Ofiyok) to unparalleled heights.

From the arid plains to the fertile valleys, Sudan's economic renaissance unfolds, shedding the shackles of the past and embracing a future brimming with boundless opportunities. Our aspirations extend beyond mere survival, for we envision a thriving economy that nurtures and empowers every Sudanese citizen, leaving none behind.

Laying the Foundation, our first step, entails establishing a solid framework rooted in stability and sustainability. Recognizing the lessons of the past, we forge ahead with comprehensive legal and regulatory reforms that attract local and foreign investors alike, fostering an environment ripe for economic growth and innovation. Embracing the spirit of entrepreneurship, we cultivate a culture that celebrates risk-taking and rewards bold ideas.

Harnessing the rich tapestry of Sudan's natural resources becomes our next endeavor. From the precious minerals hidden beneath the earth's surface to the vast expanses of fertile land, we tap into these bountiful gifts, mindful of our responsibility to protect the environment for generations to come. By inviting responsible investment in sectors such as mining, agriculture, and oil, we unleash the potential for unprecedented prosperity that will benefit every Sudanese soul.

The journey towards economic greatness is one of diversification and industry development. No longer shall we rely on the limitations of a single industry. With unwavering determination, we embark on a path that encourages the growth of diverse sectors, manufacturing, and industrial prowess. By nurturing local production and fostering export-oriented industries, we will create a thriving economy that brims with innovation and job opportunities.

But our progress extends beyond the tangible. It is intrinsically linked to the development of our infrastructure and connectivity. As bridges rise, roads expand, and ports flourish, Sudan assumes its rightful place on the world stage. We invest in sustainable and modern transportation networks, powered by renewable energy sources, to foster seamless trade and regional integration. Through robust telecommunications and digital infrastructure, we enable Sudanese ingenuity to connect with the global marketplace.

This economic awakening is incomplete without the empowerment of our greatest resource: our people. With a renewed focus on human capital development, we invest in education and vocational training programs that equip our workforce with the skills demanded by emerging industries.

We nurture a spirit of curiosity and discovery, encouraging research and development to drive innovation. By ensuring access to quality healthcare and social services, we cultivate a vibrant society where every individual thrives.

In this journey, Sudan does not stand alone. We extend our hand in friendship to the international community, forging meaningful partnerships and trade relations. By leveraging our strategic location and embracing fair economic agreements, we create a win-win scenario that propels Sudan's economy to new heights. Our economic resurgence reverberates beyond borders, contributing to regional stability and global prosperity.

As we embark on this transformative chapter, we stand on the precipice of a future where Sudan's economic might radiates across the globe. With resolute determination, we march forward, propelled by the ideals of innovation, sustainability, and inclusivity. Join us as we unravel the tapestry of Sudan's economic renaissance, where dreams become realities and prosperity knows no bounds.

## Laying the Foundation - Building a Strong Economic Framework

As I envision the transformation of Sudan's economy, I am acutely aware of the need to lay a sturdy foundation upon which prosperity can flourish. This first section explores the crucial elements that form the bedrock of our economic resurgence, instilling stability, sustainability, and a conducive environment for growth.

To realize our dreams, we must draw valuable lessons from the past. Reflecting on the economic struggles and setbacks that once plagued us, we understand the significance of stability as a prerequisite for sustainable development. Thus, we embark on a path guided by prudent economic policies that strike a balance between growth and long-term resilience.

Central to this endeavor is the establishment of a robust legal and regulatory framework that inspires confidence in investors. We recognize that attracting both local and foreign investment is essential to fueling economic expansion and job creation. By modernizing our laws, streamlining bureaucratic processes, and ensuring transparency, we send a clear message to the global community: Sudan is open for business.

Embracing the spirit of entrepreneurship, we cultivate a culture that celebrates innovation, risk-taking, and the transformative power of ideas. We recognize that economic growth is not solely dependent on external factors but also on the ingenuity and determination of our own people. Through targeted programs and incentives, we encourage the birth of startups and the nurturing of small and medium-sized enterprises (SMEs) that will form the backbone of Sudan's economic landscape.

Education and knowledge are the fuel that drives progress. Therefore, we prioritize investing in quality education and vocational training programs that equip our workforce with the skills demanded by emerging industries. By empowering our people with the tools they need to thrive in the digital age, we ensure that Sudan remains competitive on a global scale. Furthermore, we encourage a spirit of lifelong learning and foster an environment that celebrates research and development, where ideas are nurtured and transformed into tangible innovations.

Sustainability is not merely a buzzword; it is a fundamental pillar of our economic vision. We recognize the delicate balance between economic growth and environmental preservation. With responsible resource management, we strive to harness Sudan's abundant natural resources without compromising the well-being of future generations. By embracing renewable energy sources and adopting eco-friendly practices, we lay the groundwork for a greener and more sustainable future.

The foundation we build extends beyond economic considerations. It encompasses the principles of social justice, inclusivity, and equal opportunities for all. We understand that a prosperous nation is one that values its citizens, providing them with access to quality healthcare, social services, and a dignified standard of living. By nurturing a society that thrives on diversity and inclusivity, we unlock the full potential of every Sudanese individual, ensuring that no one is left behind.

When we look deeply into it, we invite both Sudanese and the international community to join hands in building a strong economic foundation. Through collaboration and partnership, we can leverage our collective strengths to propel Sudan's economy to new heights. Together, we will forge a path that leads to economic prosperity, where the dreams and visions I hold dear become a living reality for every Sudanese citizen.

Furthermore, we will explore how we harness Sudan's rich natural resources, diversify our industries, enhance infrastructure and connectivity, develop our human capital, and forge strategic alliances with the global community. Together, these elements will weave the tapestry of a thriving economy, where the aspirations of Sudan's Humanity (Ofiyok) blossom into a remarkable story of triumph and progress.

## Harnessing Natural Resources - Unleashing the Potential

Looking into the abundant natural resources that grace the lands of Sudan, and the immense potential they hold for driving our economic growth. With a deep appreciation for our country's bountiful endowments, we embark on a journey to harness these resources responsibly, sustainably, and for the benefit of all Sudanese.

**Embracing Our Agricultural Heritage:** Sudan's fertile soil and favorable climate have long made it an agricultural haven. As we look to the future, I believe in unlocking the full potential of our agricultural sector. By adopting modern farming practices, investing in research and development, and supporting farmers with advanced techniques and tools, we can increase productivity, ensure food security, and tap into the vast opportunities that lie within our fields.

**Unlocking Mineral Wealth:** Beneath the surface of our land lies a treasure trove of mineral wealth waiting to be unleashed. Sudan boasts significant reserves of gold, copper, iron ore, and other precious minerals. Through responsible mining practices, we will extract these resources while prioritizing environmental preservation and the welfare of local communities. By attracting responsible mining companies and fostering a favorable investment climate, we can create a thriving mining industry that benefits both the nation and its people.

**Tapping into Energy Resources:** Energy is the lifeblood of any thriving economy. Sudan possesses immense potential in renewable energy sources, such as solar and wind power, thanks to our abundant sunlight and favorable wind patterns. By investing in renewable energy infrastructure and incentivizing clean energy projects, we can reduce our dependence on fossil fuels, promote sustainable development, and position Sudan as a regional leader in the green energy revolution.

**Water Resources Management:** Water is a precious resource that holds tremendous economic value. Sudan is blessed with the Nile River, the lifeline of our nation, and other water bodies that offer immense potential for irrigation, hydropower generation, and transportation. Through strategic water resources management, including the construction of reservoirs, dams, and irrigation systems, we can optimize water usage, enhance agricultural productivity, and provide clean water to our growing population.

**Preserving Biodiversity and Eco-Tourism:** Sudan's rich biodiversity, including its diverse wildlife and pristine natural habitats, is a unique asset that has the potential to drive eco-tourism and sustainable economic growth. By establishing protected areas, promoting responsible tourism practices, and raising awareness about the importance of conservation, we can showcase Sudan's natural beauty to the world while preserving our ecological heritage for future generations.

**Value Addition and Export:** Unlocking the true potential of our natural resources requires not only their extraction but also value addition and efficient export strategies. By investing in processing and refining industries, we can transform raw materials into higher-value finished products, creating job opportunities and increasing export revenues. Additionally, by forging strategic partnerships and trade agreements with global markets, we can ensure a steady demand for our products and maximize the economic benefits of our natural resources.

Together, we will unlock the wealth that lies within Sudan's borders, ensuring that our economic progress is sustainable, inclusive, and beneficial to every Sudanese citizen.

# Empowering Industries for Economic Growth

By fostering a conducive environment for innovation, investment, and entrepreneurship, we can cultivate a vibrant and diverse industrial sector that generates employment opportunities, fosters technological advancements, and enhances our global competitiveness.

**Promoting Industrial Diversification**: I firmly believe in the power of industrial diversification to propel our economy forward. We must move beyond traditional sectors and encourage the development of new industries that align with global trends and emerging markets. By identifying and supporting sectors with high growth potential, such as information technology, renewable energy, manufacturing, and creative industries, we can create a diverse economic landscape that reduces our reliance on a single industry and enhances our resilience in the face of global challenges.

**Investing in Infrastructure:** The foundation of a robust industrial sector lies in a well-developed infrastructure network. We must prioritize investment in transportation, energy, telecommunications, and logistics infrastructure to provide a solid backbone for industrial growth. By improving connectivity within and beyond our borders, we can facilitate the movement of goods, reduce costs, and attract both domestic and foreign investment.

**Enhancing Access to Finance:** Access to finance is crucial for entrepreneurs and businesses to start and expand their operations. In this chapter, we will explore strategies to enhance access to capital, including the establishment of specialized financial institutions, the promotion of venture capital and angel investor networks, and the development of innovative financing models. By facilitating access to finance, we can empower aspiring entrepreneurs, stimulate innovation, and fuel the growth of small and medium-sized enterprises (SMEs).

**Fostering Innovation and Research:** Innovation and research are catalysts for economic transformation. We must create an ecosystem that nurtures innovation, encourages research and development, and supports technology transfer. By establishing research and innovation hubs, partnering with academic institutions, and incentivizing collaboration between the private sector and academia, we can drive technological advancements, foster a culture of innovation, and create a pipeline of skilled professionals.

**Strengthening Business Environment and Regulatory Framework:** A favorable business environment and a transparent regulatory framework are essential for attracting investment and fostering entrepreneurship. In this section, we will discuss the importance of streamlining bureaucratic processes, reducing red tape, and ensuring the rule of law. By creating a business-friendly environment characterized by fairness, transparency, and ease of doing business, we can attract domestic and foreign investors, stimulate economic activity, and create employment opportunities.

**Promoting International Trade and Investment:** Sudan's integration into the global economy is crucial for sustainable economic growth. We must actively engage in international trade and investment by pursuing trade agreements, fostering economic partnerships, and participating in regional and global economic organizations. By expanding market access for Sudanese products and services, we can boost exports, attract foreign direct investment, and create a favorable environment for trade and investment.

By nurturing a vibrant and competitive industrial sector, we can create a sustainable foundation for long-term economic growth, improve living standards, and provide opportunities for all Sudanese citizens to thrive in a dynamic and inclusive economy.

## Infrastructure and Connectivity

By investing in robust infrastructure networks and fostering seamless connectivity, we can unlock the full potential of our nation, facilitate trade and commerce, and enhance the overall quality of life for our people.

**Modernizing Transportation Systems:** Efficient transportation systems are the lifelines of economic development. To propel Sudan forward, we must modernize our transportation infrastructure, including roadways, railways, airports, and ports. By investing in the expansion and improvement of our transportation networks, we can facilitate the movement of goods and people, reduce transportation costs, and enhance our regional and international connectivity.

**Developing Digital Infrastructure:** In today's interconnected world, digital infrastructure plays a pivotal role in driving economic growth and fostering innovation. We must prioritize the development of reliable and high-speed internet connectivity across the nation, ensuring that even remote areas have access to the digital world. By bridging the digital divide and promoting digital literacy, we can empower our citizens, enable e-commerce and digital entrepreneurship, and attract digital industries that contribute to job creation and economic diversification.

**Harnessing Renewable Energy:** The transition to clean and sustainable energy sources is not only essential for mitigating climate change but also presents tremendous economic opportunities. Sudan is blessed with abundant solar and wind resources, which we must harness to generate clean and affordable energy. By investing in renewable energy infrastructure, we can reduce our dependence on fossil fuels, create jobs in the renewable energy sector, and become a regional leader in clean energy production.

**Expanding Water and Sanitation Systems:** Access to clean water and adequate sanitation is a fundamental human right and a prerequisite for economic development. In this section, we will explore strategies to expand and improve our water and sanitation infrastructure, ensuring that all Sudanese communities have access to safe drinking water and proper sanitation facilities. By addressing water scarcity, promoting sustainable water management practices, and improving sanitation standards, we can enhance public health, boost agricultural productivity, and create a more resilient society.

**Strengthening Energy Infrastructure:** Reliable and affordable energy is the backbone of industrial growth and economic productivity. We must invest in modernizing our energy infrastructure, including power generation, transmission, and distribution systems. By diversifying our energy sources and improving energy efficiency, we can ensure a stable and sustainable energy supply for households, businesses, and industries, thereby driving economic development and attracting investment.

**Enhancing Regional and International Connectivity:** Sudan's geographical location positions us as a gateway to Africa and the Middle East. To fully leverage this advantage, we must enhance our regional and international connectivity through the development of efficient transportation links, including air, land, and sea routes. By promoting regional integration, facilitating cross-border trade, and attracting foreign investment, we can position Sudan as a regional economic hub and unlock new opportunities for growth and prosperity.

Delving into these infrastructure and connectivity initiatives, highlighting the specific projects and policies that will shape Sudan's economic landscape. By prioritizing infrastructure development and ensuring seamless connectivity, we can create an enabling environment for businesses, improve access to markets, stimulate economic activity, and ultimately improve the lives of all Sudanese citizens. Together, we will build a modern and interconnected Sudan that thrives in the global arena.

**Human Capital Development**

In this section, I highlight the importance of investing in human capital as the cornerstone of Sudan's progress and prosperity. By prioritizing education, healthcare, and skills development, we can unleash the full potential of our people and create a workforce that is skilled, innovative, and adaptable to the demands of a rapidly evolving global economy.

**Transforming Education:** Education is the key to unlocking individual potential and driving societal progress. We must embark on a transformative journey to revitalize our education system, ensuring access to quality education for all Sudanese children, regardless of their background or location. By investing in modern educational infrastructure, providing professional development opportunities for teachers, and embracing innovative teaching methods, we can equip our youth with the knowledge, skills, and values they need to succeed in the 21st century.

**Promoting Technical and Vocational Training:** To foster economic growth and address the demands of a changing job market, we must emphasize technical and vocational training. By expanding access to technical education and vocational training programs, we can equip individuals with practical skills that align with industry needs. This will not only empower young people to enter the workforce with confidence but also promote entrepreneurship and job creation, driving economic diversification and reducing unemployment rates.

**Enhancing Healthcare Services:** A healthy population is a productive population. We must prioritize the development and improvement of healthcare infrastructure, ensuring access to quality healthcare services for all Sudanese citizens. By expanding healthcare facilities, training healthcare professionals, and adopting preventive healthcare measures, we can enhance public health outcomes, reduce the burden of disease, and improve the overall well-being of our people. Investing in healthcare also contributes to social and economic equity, as healthy individuals are better able to contribute to the nation's progress.

**Fostering Research and Innovation:** To thrive in the global knowledge economy, we must foster a culture of research and innovation. By creating an enabling environment for research and development, we can encourage scientific discoveries, technological advancements, and entrepreneurial ventures. Investing in research institutions, supporting collaboration between academia and industry, and incentivizing innovation will drive economic growth, attract investment, and position Sudan as a hub for innovation and creativity.

**Empowering Women and Youth:** The empowerment of women and youth is crucial for Sudan's development. We must create opportunities that enable women to fully participate in all sectors of the economy and assume leadership roles. By promoting gender equality, supporting women entrepreneurs, and ensuring access to education and healthcare, we can unlock the untapped potential of half of our population. Similarly, we must invest in our youth, providing them with the skills, mentorship, and opportunities they need to become agents of change and contribute to the nation's progress.

**Embracing Lifelong Learning:** Learning should be a lifelong journey. We must encourage a culture of continuous learning and upskilling, enabling individuals to adapt to technological advancements and evolving market demands. By promoting adult education programs, vocational training opportunities, and professional development initiatives, we can ensure that our workforce remains competitive and our people have the tools they need to thrive in a rapidly changing world.

Exploring these pillars of human capital development, highlighting the specific strategies and initiatives that will shape Sudan's future. By investing in education, healthcare, skills development, and research, we can empower our people, unleash their potential, and create a society that is equipped to navigate the challenges and seize the opportunities of the 21st century. This way, we can build a skilled, healthy, and innovative workforce that will drive Sudan's progress and secure a prosperous future for all.

## Foreign Relations and Trade

We must know the importance of fostering strong foreign relations and expanding our international trade partnerships. By engaging with the global community and leveraging our unique resources and potential, we can open doors to new opportunities, attract foreign investment, and establish Sudan as a respected player in the international arena.

**Building Diplomatic Relationships:** Diplomacy plays a crucial role in shaping our foreign relations. We must actively engage with other nations, promoting dialogue, understanding, and cooperation. By building strong diplomatic relationships, we can foster mutual trust and respect, paving the way for collaboration in various fields, including trade, investment, security, and cultural exchange. A diplomatic approach will help us navigate regional and global challenges, representing Sudan's interests effectively on the international stage.

**Strengthening Regional Cooperation:** As a nation situated in a region of immense diversity and potential, we must foster closer ties with our neighboring countries. By strengthening regional cooperation, we can harness shared resources, promote stability, and stimulate economic growth. Collaborative efforts in areas such as infrastructure development, energy, trade facilitation, and joint investment ventures can create a regional ecosystem of prosperity, benefitting all participating nations.

**Attracting Foreign Investment:** To realize our economic aspirations, we must actively attract foreign investment. By creating an investor-friendly environment, offering incentives, and streamlining regulatory processes, we can encourage international businesses to establish a presence in Sudan. Foreign direct investment brings not only capital but also technology transfer, job creation, and market access, stimulating economic growth and diversification. Through strategic partnerships, we can leverage the expertise and resources of foreign investors to catalyze our development.

**Promoting Export-Oriented Industries:** Expanding our export capacity is vital for reducing trade imbalances and generating foreign exchange earnings. We must identify and develop sectors with high export potential, such as agriculture, mining, manufacturing, and tourism. By investing in infrastructure, improving logistics, and adopting quality standards, we can enhance the competitiveness of Sudanese products in international markets. Moreover, strategic marketing campaigns and participation in trade fairs and exhibitions will help showcase the quality and uniqueness of our goods and services to the world.

**Facilitating Trade Agreements:** Entering into trade agreements with other nations is crucial for expanding our market access and ensuring fair trade practices. We must actively engage in negotiations to establish bilateral and multilateral trade agreements that benefit Sudanese exporters and importers. These agreements can lower trade barriers, promote tariff reductions, and facilitate the movement of goods and services across borders. By embracing international trade rules and regulations, we can foster a conducive environment for trade and position Sudan as a reliable trading partner.

**Cultural and Educational Exchanges:** Promoting cultural and educational exchanges with other countries is instrumental in building understanding, fostering people-to-people connections, and enhancing our global reputation. By encouraging student exchanges, cultural festivals, and artistic collaborations, we can showcase the richness of Sudanese culture, traditions, and talents. These exchanges not only contribute to cultural diversity but also open doors for economic collaboration, tourism, and knowledge sharing, strengthening our position on the world stage.

The significance of nurturing foreign relations, attracting foreign investment, and expanding our global trade networks, embrace diplomacy, regional cooperation, and strategic partnerships, we can position Sudan as a key player in the international arena. Through trade promotion, export diversification, and participation in global economic initiatives, we will enhance our economic growth and create opportunities for our people. Together, we will forge strong bonds with the international community, realizing the full potential of Sudan and securing a prosperous future for our nation.

As I conclude this transformative journey through the chapters of Sudan's revival, I am filled with hope, determination, and a profound sense of pride for our nation and its people. The vision and dreams I have shared throughout this chapter are not merely idealistic fantasies but tangible possibilities that lie within our grasp. We stand on the precipice of a new era, where the dreams of a united Sudan are becoming a reality.

We have explored the foundational pillars that will propel Sudan to new heights. From the revival of our economy and the harnessing of our abundant natural resources to the development of our human capital and the forging of strong international relationships, we have laid the groundwork for a prosperous and united Sudan.

Our economy, once stagnant, is now thriving. The world recognizes the untapped potential that lies within our borders, and foreign investors are flocking to seize the opportunities that abound. We are witnessing the emergence of vibrant industries, job creation, and sustainable development that will uplift the lives of our people and empower future generations.

Our natural resources, a blessing bestowed upon us by the hands of nature, are being harnessed responsibly and sustainably. We have become stewards of our land, protecting its treasures and ensuring that future generations will inherit a bountiful legacy. The wealth of our resources has become a catalyst for economic growth, technological advancement, and environmental stewardship.

Our human capital, the driving force behind our nation's progress, is being nurtured and empowered. We have invested in education, healthcare, and skills development, recognizing that our people are our most valuable asset. With a highly educated and skilled workforce, we are poised to compete on a global stage, spearheading innovation and excellence in various fields.

Our international relations have flourished, and we have become a respected player on the world stage. Through diplomacy, regional cooperation, and strategic partnerships, we have fostered mutual understanding, collaboration, and shared prosperity. Our doors are open to the world, and we are reaping the benefits of fruitful trade, cultural exchange, and global solidarity.

Together, we have shattered the shackles of doubt and disbelief, proving that a united Sudan can rise above adversity and reclaim its rightful place among the nations of the world. We have defied the odds, embraced our potential, and charted a new course for our beloved nation.

The dreams and visions I have shared in these pages are not mine alone. They belong to all Sudanese people, past, present, and future. They are a testament to our resilience, our spirit, and our unwavering belief in the limitless possibilities that lie within us.

As I close this chapter, I invite you, my fellow Sudanese, to join hands and hearts in the pursuit of our shared dreams. Let us continue to work tirelessly, side by side, to build the Sudan we envision—a Sudan that is prosperous, united, and a shining example to the world.

The journey ahead may be challenging, but with determination, perseverance, and an unwavering commitment to our ideals, we will overcome any obstacle that stands in our way. Together, we will witness the transformation of our nation, the realization of our dreams, and the renaissance of Sudan.

In the end, it is not just about the dreams we hold within our hearts but the actions we take to turn those dreams into reality. Let us march forward, guided by the beacon of hope and unity, and together, let us redefine the destiny of Sudan.

The future is bright, and the possibilities are endless. The dreams of a united Sudan are within our reach. Let us dare to dream, let us dare to act, and let us create a legacy that will inspire generations to come.

Together, as one, we will forge a new path, a path that leads us to greatness.

## Chapter 5: Environment

Amidst the vibrant tapestry of dreams and aspirations that weave through the pages of this journey, we now turn our gaze to the awe-inspiring world that embraces Sudan - a land where nature's splendor unfolds in its purest form. Welcome to Chapter 5: Environment, where the very essence of Sudan's breathtaking landscapes and fragile ecosystems comes alive.

As we dig deeper on this exploration, imagine standing at the crossroads of untamed wilderness, where verdant forests whisper ancient tales and mighty mountains beckon us to reach for the sky. Picture yourself traversing the vast expanse of deserts, their golden dunes stretching as far as the eye can see, holding secrets yet to be unveiled.

But beneath the surface of this pristine beauty lies a crucial realization: our planet is fragile, and our actions have consequences. In this chapter, we embrace the challenge of environmental stewardship, acknowledging the vital importance of preserving Sudan's natural heritage for generations to come.

Together, we shall unravel the enchantment of Sudan's diverse ecosystems, where majestic flora and fauna reside. From the rhythmic rustle of leaves in vibrant forests to the elusive dance of sunlight on cascading waterfalls, each aspect of this precious environment holds a story waiting to be told.

Yet, amidst the magnificence, we must confront the environmental challenges that cast a shadow upon this landscape. Deforestation threatens the harmony of these ancient woodlands, while pollution seeps into once-pristine waters, leaving a mark on the delicate balance of life. Climate change casts its long-reaching tendrils, reminding us of the urgency to take action.

But fear not, for Sudan is a land where resilience thrives. In the face of adversity, environmental conservation efforts have sprouted like resilient saplings, nurturing hope and fostering change. We shall delve into the success stories, where passionate individuals, communities, and organizations have united to protect Sudan's natural treasures.

Through the lens of sustainability, we shall envision a future where economic growth and environmental protection entwine in a harmonious dance. We'll explore the avenues of sustainable development, embracing green technologies, and fostering innovation. Let us reimagine a Sudan that harnesses the power of renewable energy, where eco-tourism flourishes, and responsible practices permeate every aspect of life.

As we venture forth, remember that the future is in our hands. Let the allure of Sudan's natural wonders kindle a fire within, igniting our shared responsibility to be the guardians of this land. Together, we shall preserve its majesty, ensuring that future generations may bask in the same awe-inspiring beauty that captivates us today.

As we embark on this transformative journey through Sudan's environment, where dreams are woven into reality, and the power of collective action paves the way for a greener, more sustainable world. Embrace the call of the wild and let the wonders of Sudan's natural heritage inspire your spirit.

## The Natural Splendor of Sudan

### A. Describing the Diverse Landscapes And Ecosystems

Sudan, a land of remarkable contrasts, beckons with its awe-inspiring natural splendor. Let us embark on a journey to discover the diverse landscapes and ecosystems that make this land truly extraordinary.

**Vibrant forests and lush greenery**: Step into the heart of Sudan's enchanting forests, where sunlight filters through a canopy of towering trees, casting a dappled glow on the forest floor. Here, you'll find a treasure trove of biodiversity, as rare species of flora and fauna find sanctuary amidst this verdant tapestry. From the vibrant hues of exotic flowers to the haunting melodies of elusive birds, these forests hold a symphony of life waiting to be discovered.

**Majestic mountains and breathtaking valleys**: Sudan's majestic mountains rise proudly, their peaks reaching towards the heavens. Traverse rugged slopes adorned with hardy vegetation, where resilient wildlife has made a home against all odds. As you stand at the summit, breathtaking vistas unfold before your eyes, revealing sweeping valleys carved by ancient rivers. Witness the ever-changing play of light and shadow as the sun kisses the landscape, illuminating a world of sublime beauty.

**Expansive deserts and their unique beauty**: The deserts of Sudan possess a mystical allure, where vast stretches of golden sands stretch beyond the horizon. In this arid wilderness, life finds a way to thrive against adversity. Marvel at the artistry of wind-sculpted dunes, their graceful curves offering an ethereal backdrop. Discover the resilience of desert flora and fauna, adapted to survive in this harsh and unforgiving environment. As the night unfolds, behold a celestial spectacle as countless stars blanket the desert sky, igniting a sense of wonder within.

**B. Highlighting the Rich Biodiversity and Unique Wildlife**

Sudan is a haven for biodiversity, teeming with a remarkable array of wildlife that calls this land home. Within its borders, you'll encounter extraordinary species, each contributing to the delicate balance of nature.

**Iconic species and their significance:** From the regal African elephant majestically roaming the savannahs to the agile cheetah sprinting across the grasslands, Sudan's iconic species capture the essence of this diverse land. Behold the grace of the towering giraffe, the raw power of the African lion, and the elusive beauty of the African leopard. Each species holds a significant place in Sudan's natural heritage, symbolizing strength, resilience, and interconnectedness.

**Endangered species and the need for conservation efforts:** Sadly, Sudan also harbors species on the brink of extinction, their survival hanging in the balance. Witness the gentle giants of the African rhinoceros, battling against relentless poaching. Marvel at the delicate grace of the slender-horned gazelle, fighting for survival in a changing landscape. It is within our hands to safeguard these precious creatures, to protect their habitats, and to champion conservation efforts that offer them a fighting chance.

As we delve deeper into Sudan's natural wonders, let us recognize the importance of preserving these delicate ecosystems and nurturing the incredible biodiversity that thrives within. We can ensure that future generations continue to marvel at the vibrant forests, majestic mountains, and expansive deserts that define the natural splendor of Sudan.

## Environmental Challenges Faced

Sudan's natural landscapes and ecosystems confront the environmental challenges that cast a shadow upon this land of enchantment. These challenges serve as a call to action, urging us to preserve the delicate balance of nature for the generations to come.

**Addressing the Impact of Human Activities:**

Human activities have left their mark on Sudan's natural environment, posing significant threats to its vitality. The consequences of these actions reverberate through the intricate web of life, demanding our attention and concerted efforts for change.

Deforestation stands as a formidable challenge, as swathes of precious forests are lost to logging, agriculture, and urban expansion. The loss of these vital habitats not only disrupts the delicate balance of ecosystems but also robs countless species of their homes and food sources.

Pollution, another pressing concern, seeps into Sudan's rivers, lakes, and oceans, contaminating the very sources of life. Industrial waste, agricultural runoff, and improper waste disposal contribute to the degradation of water quality, endangering aquatic life and compromising the health of both humans and wildlife.

Perhaps the most far-reaching challenge of all is climate change. Rising temperatures, erratic weather patterns, and sea-level rise threaten Sudan's diverse ecosystems. The delicate balance that sustains life is disrupted, leading to altered habitats, species migrations, and the potential loss of valuable biodiversity.

## Exploring the Importance of Sustainable Practices:

To address these environmental challenges, we must embrace sustainable practices that harmonize human development with the preservation of Sudan's natural heritage. It is within our power to mitigate the impacts of our actions and foster a more sustainable future.

Conservation of natural resources stands as a paramount endeavor. By promoting responsible consumption, minimizing waste, and safeguarding critical resources such as freshwater and fertile soil, we can ensure their availability for future generations.

The adoption of renewable energy sources serves as a catalyst for change. Embracing solar, wind, and hydropower energy systems can reduce reliance on fossil fuels, curbing greenhouse gas emissions and mitigating the effects of climate change.

Waste management and recycling initiatives hold immense potential to minimize the burden on Sudan's environment. By implementing comprehensive waste management systems, we can reduce pollution, recycle valuable materials, and embrace a circular economy that minimizes waste generation.

It is essential to educate and raise awareness about the significance of sustainable practices among individuals and communities. Through environmental education programs and community engagement, we can empower Sudanese citizens to become stewards of their environment, fostering a culture of sustainability.

By acknowledging these environmental challenges and embracing sustainable practices, we lay the foundation for a brighter and greener future. The path ahead is not without obstacles, but united in our resolve, we can transform the challenges we face into opportunities for positive change.

The remarkable environmental conservation efforts that have taken root in Sudan, celebrating the successes and highlighting the individuals and organizations dedicated to protecting Sudan's natural treasures. Together, we can build a sustainable future where the marvels of Sudan's environment endure for generations to come.

## Environmental Conservation Efforts

As we journey through the landscapes of Sudan and confront the environmental challenges it faces, we are met with a glimmer of hope. Across this remarkable land, environmental conservation efforts have taken root, nurturing a vision of a sustainable future. Let us explore the remarkable initiatives and the passionate individuals driving change.

### Showcasing Successful Initiatives and Projects

Sudan is home to an array of successful environmental conservation initiatives that inspire and demonstrate the power of collective action. These endeavors have flourished, protecting vital ecosystems and preserving Sudan's natural treasures.

Preservation of national parks and protected areas stands as a testament to Sudan's commitment to conservation. These sanctuaries provide a haven for diverse flora and fauna, ensuring the long-term survival of endangered species and safeguarding critical habitats.

Reforestation programs and afforestation campaigns have taken root, rejuvenating landscapes once marred by deforestation. By planting new trees and restoring degraded areas, Sudanese communities and organizations contribute to the revival of forests and the mitigation of climate change.

Efforts in wildlife conservation and anti-poaching measures play a pivotal role in protecting Sudan's unique biodiversity. These initiatives combine education, law enforcement, and community engagement to combat illegal wildlife trade and preserve threatened species.

**Empowering Local Communities and Raising Awareness**

Environmental conservation thrives when communities are empowered and engaged. Sudanese citizens have taken on the responsibility of protecting their natural heritage, understanding the interconnectedness between environmental health and their own well-being.

Environmental education and awareness programs play a critical role in fostering a sense of stewardship among

Sudanese communities. By promoting knowledge about the value of nature, these initiatives inspire individuals to actively participate in conservation efforts and make sustainable choices.

Citizen participation in conservation activities is encouraged through community-led initiatives. From volunteer clean-up campaigns to sustainable agriculture practices, Sudanese communities come together, embracing their role as custodians of the environment.

Collaboration with international organizations strengthens Sudan's conservation efforts. By partnering with global initiatives, Sudan gains access to expertise, resources, and funding, enhancing the impact of local conservation projects.

Through these collective efforts, Sudan is cultivating a culture of environmental consciousness and action, transforming the challenges into opportunities for a sustainable future.

There are many stories of these conservation pioneers, unveiling their passion, resilience, and the lasting impact of their endeavors. We celebrate the triumphs and learn from the lessons these projects offer, inspiring a new generation of Sudanese environmental stewards.

The journey continues as we explore the path towards sustainable development and envision a future where Sudan's natural heritage thrives hand-in-hand with human progress. Join us as we forge ahead, united in our determination to protect Sudan's environment and preserve its wonders for generations to come.

## Sustainable Development and Future Prospects

As we navigate the landscapes of Sudan and witness the remarkable environmental conservation efforts, a vision of sustainable development emerges. Sudan is poised to embark on a transformative journey, where economic growth and environmental protection intertwine harmoniously. Let us explore the path towards a brighter and greener future.

### Embracing the Integration of Environmental Sustainability

Balancing economic growth and environmental protection is essential for Sudan's sustainable development. By integrating environmental considerations into various sectors, Sudan can pave the way for a resilient and thriving future.

Green infrastructure and sustainable urban planning offer a blueprint for creating environmentally friendly cities and communities. By embracing concepts such as energy-efficient buildings, accessible public transportation, and green spaces, Sudan can foster a high quality of life while minimizing its ecological footprint.

Promoting eco-tourism and responsible travel unlocks the potential to showcase Sudan's natural wonders while preserving them for generations to come. Sustainable tourism practices, such as promoting local culture, supporting community-based initiatives, and preserving fragile ecosystems, can ensure that Sudan's natural heritage remains intact while benefiting local communities.

**Envisioning a Brighter and Greener Future**

Sudan has the opportunity to harness renewable energy sources and reduce its dependence on fossil fuels. By embracing solar, wind, and hydropower, Sudan can not only mitigate the impacts of climate change but also foster energy independence and unlock new avenues for economic growth.

Implementing green technologies and practices across industries is crucial for sustainable development. From agriculture to manufacturing, Sudan can adopt eco-friendly practices, such as efficient irrigation systems, sustainable waste management, and resource-efficient production methods, reducing its environmental footprint and enhancing productivity.

Embracing innovation and research for sustainable solutions will drive Sudan's progress towards a greener future. By investing in research and development, Sudan can unlock new technologies, processes, and solutions that promote sustainability, addressing environmental challenges and fueling economic growth simultaneously.

In this journey towards sustainable development, Sudan must recognize the importance of stakeholder collaboration. Government bodies, businesses, communities, and individuals must unite, sharing knowledge, resources, and expertise, to collectively shape a sustainable future.

We must aim to create a Sudan that thrives against all odds. A Sudan where renewable energy powers its cities, green infrastructure fosters vibrant communities, and responsible practices permeate every aspect of life. Let us embrace this vision, charting a course towards a future that balances progress and preservation.

The journey continues, fueled by the shared commitment to create a Sudan that flourishes economically, socially, and environmentally. Soon, we will be able to forge a path towards a sustainable future that showcases the wonders of Sudan while safeguarding its natural heritage for generations to come.

As our journey through the dreams and visions for Sudan reaches its culmination, we find ourselves at a crossroads of hope and determination. The transformation of Sudan from the depths of adversity to the pinnacle of triumph lies within our grasp. We must pave the way for a Sudan that transcends boundaries and soars to new heights.

In this chapter, we have embarked on a remarkable odyssey, exploring the boundless potential of Sudan's humanity and land. From the lofty peaks of idealism to the fertile valleys of progress, we have woven a tapestry of dreams, united by the thread of unwavering belief.

Sudan, a land that rises from the very bottom to the top of the totem pole, stands poised to rewrite its destiny. It is a country endowed with remarkable resources, be they spiritual or materialistic, awaiting our embrace. We have witnessed the wonders that lie within our grasp, and now it is time to seize them.

Our journey has taken us through the realms of education, justice, freedom, and unity, each chapter unveiling a facet of Sudan's grand tapestry. The environment, too, holds a pivotal role in shaping our shared future. It is a call to protect, preserve, and nurture the natural heritage that has long been our source of inspiration.

As we reflect upon the challenges we face, let us remember that Sudan's path to prosperity is illuminated by the power of unity, determination, and sustainability. It is a journey that demands the collective efforts of each and every one of us, from the grassroots to the halls of power.

Together, we shall embrace the integration of environmental sustainability, creating a harmonious balance between economic growth and the protection of our precious natural resources. Let us forge ahead with green technologies, sustainable practices, and a deep-rooted commitment to responsible development.

In the heart of Sudan, we find the strength to overcome adversity and the resilience to transform dreams into reality. We carry within us the spirit of our ancestors, the hope of our children, and the dreams of a united nation. We are the architects of our destiny, guided by the ideals of progress, justice, and love for our humanity.

As we close this chapter, let the words of unity, progress, and resilience echo in our hearts. Let them serve as a beacon of inspiration, reminding us of the limitless possibilities that await us. Sudan, our beloved land, holds the key to a future that transcends the boundaries of imagination.

Together, hand in hand, let us build a Sudan where dreams become achievements, where prosperity is shared by all, and where the echoes of our triumphs resound throughout the world. Sudan, a nation on the rise, a land of boundless potential, and a testament to the indomitable spirit of its people.

The journey continues, propelled by the power of our dreams, the strength of our unity, and the unwavering belief in the radiant future that lies ahead. Sudan, our Sudan, shall flourish, illuminating the path for generations to come.

This is our destiny, this is our legacy. May Sudan rise, may our humanity thrive, and may our dreams become a resplendent reality.

*Together, united, Sudan shall prevail!*

# Chapter 6: Leadership

Leadership is the compass that guides a nation through the tempests of history. It's the flame that ignites transformation and the force that propels societies from obscurity to greatness. As I reflect on the journey that lies ahead for the Humanity of Sudan (Ofiyok), I am reminded of the words of John F. Kennedy, *"Leadership and learning are indispensable to each other."* Our journey is not just about moving forward; it's about forging a new path, guided by visionary ideals that will shape the destiny of a nation.

From the depths of adversity, Sudan rises, fueled by a spirit of unyielding hope and a vision of a brighter future. In this chapter of our nation's story, we cast aside the limitations of the past and embrace the limitless potential that lies within us. Our journey to leadership isn't just a pursuit of power; it's a commitment to ushering in an era of unprecedented progress, where every Sudanese individual contributes to the collective tapestry of success.

In the pages that follow, we'll delve into the very essence of visionary leadership – the art of seeing beyond the horizon, of inspiring change, and of embracing diversity to cultivate unity. One must know how nurturing homegrown leaders, fostering inclusivity, and embracing the power of education will act as catalysts for our ascent to greatness. Alongside these principles, we'll uncover the bedrock of ethical conduct that supports good governance, and how collaboration and diplomacy will define our global influence.

We find ourselves at the crossroads of history, where the torch of leadership passes from one generation to the next. Our path isn't simply guided by the present moment, but by the dreams and visions we carry for the generations that will follow. In the words of Nelson Mandela, *"A leader is like a shepherd. He stays behind the flock, letting the most nimble go out ahead, whereupon the others follow, not realizing that all along they are being directed from behind."* Our leaders, guided by a shared vision and unwavering purpose, will lead us toward a future where Sudan shines as a beacon of progress, harmony, and prosperity.

*"The best way to predict the future is to create it."*

- Peter Drucker

## Visionary Leadership for Transformation

In the heart of visionary leadership lies the power to transform. It's a leadership that isn't confined to the present, but stretches its arms towards a future unseen, driven by a compelling vision that resonates with the aspirations of a nation. Visionary leaders possess the ability to look beyond immediate challenges, to peer into the horizon and imagine possibilities that others might overlook.

Foresight becomes their guiding star, as they navigate the complexities of societal progress. Courageously breaking away from the status quo, they step onto uncharted territories, knowing that only by daring to dream differently can transformation be achieved. This courage is infectious, inspiring a collective sense of purpose among the people, as they rally around a shared dream, united by the hope of a better tomorrow.

Yet, visionary leadership isn't just about bold leaps. Empathy flows at its core, allowing leaders to understand the needs, aspirations, and fears of the very people they serve. This empathy fuels a genuine connection, cultivating trust and a deep sense of belonging within the nation. Adaptability complements this empathy, as visionary leaders recognize that the journey to transformation isn't linear; it's a dynamic process that requires constant recalibration in response to shifting circumstances.

History has borne witness to the immense impact of visionary leaders. From Martin Luther King Jr.'s dream of racial equality to Nelson Mandela's pursuit of a unified South Africa, their visions reverberated through time, shaping the destinies of nations. These leaders show us that the potential for progress is limitless when coupled with a potent vision, a dedication to transformative action, and an unwavering commitment to uplift their people.

As we look to Sudan's future, we find ourselves at a juncture where visionary leadership can steer our nation toward unprecedented heights. It's a leadership that doesn't succumb to the weight of challenges, but rather harnesses them as stepping stones to progress. We must explore the practical manifestations of visionary leadership, the ways it empowers our youth, bridges divides, and becomes the compass guiding us through the intricate web of modern geopolitics.

This isn't just about leaders and followers; it's about a collective journey of growth, spurred by the visionary ideals that burn in the hearts of the people. Together, we'll breathe life into the dreams that elevate Sudan from its past struggles, propelling us into a future where every milestone achieved is a testament to the power of visionary leadership.

## Nurturing Homegrown Leaders

In the rich soil of Sudan, a new generation of leaders is sprouting, ready to take on the mantle of transformation. These leaders aren't forged in distant lands; they're homegrown, shaped by the very landscape and culture they seek to uplift. Nurturing local leadership isn't just a choice; it's a necessity for our nation's progress.

Identifying these budding leaders is a process that demands keen observation and a commitment to tapping into the potential that often lies hidden beneath the surface. We must mentor and empower these individuals, we should provide them with the tools to rise beyond their circumstances, armed with the capacity to shape the trajectory of our nation.

The journey to leadership isn't solitary; it's a communal endeavor. Emerging leaders aren't just guided by their own aspirations, but by the collective dreams of the Sudanese people. In nurturing homegrown leaders, we acknowledge that each individual has a unique story, a unique path that adds to the tapestry of our national narrative.

Investment in education becomes a cornerstone of this nurturing process. By providing accessible and quality education, we equip future leaders with the intellectual foundation to tackle complex challenges. We cultivate critical thinking and encourage a curiosity that seeks to question the status quo and seek innovative solutions.

Moreover, mentorship becomes the bridge that connects the wisdom of experienced leaders with the fresh perspectives of those just stepping onto the leadership stage. This passing of the torch isn't just about knowledge transfer; it's about fostering a sense of continuity, where the lessons of the past meet the aspirations of the future.

As these homegrown leaders rise, they bring with them a deep connection to the people and the land. This rootedness translates into a leadership that is grounded in the realities of Sudan's diverse communities, resonating with their hopes and addressing their concerns. It's leadership that bridges the gap between the grassroots and the government, ensuring that policies are not just imposed but developed in collaboration with the very people they impact.

We should read the success stories of individuals who, like seeds planted in fertile soil, have grown into beacons of leadership. Through their journey, we'll witness how the nurturing of homegrown leaders isn't just a path to progress; it's a testament to the resilience and potential that define our nation's spirit. Together, we cultivate a garden of leaders, each one a testament to the boundless potential that resides within the hearts and minds of the Sudanese people.

## Inclusivity and Diversity in Leadership

In the grand tapestry of Sudan, diversity weaves a complex and beautiful pattern. Recognizing the strength that lies within this diversity, visionary leadership extends its arms to embrace inclusivity. It understands that leadership isn't confined to a singular voice; it's a harmonious symphony of perspectives, backgrounds, and experiences.

Inclusive leadership isn't just a token gesture; it's a commitment to giving every Sudanese individual a seat at the table. It means breaking down barriers that have historically excluded women, minorities, and marginalized groups. It acknowledges that the solution to our nation's challenges is found in the collaborative efforts of every citizen, irrespective of their gender, ethnicity, or social standing.

The power of inclusive leadership lies in its ability to harness the strength of diverse viewpoints. When leaders represent a wide array of backgrounds, they can draw from a reservoir of experiences that enrich decision-making and policy formulation. This diversity of thought fosters innovative solutions and helps identify blind spots that might otherwise be overlooked.

In this pursuit of inclusivity, Sudan's leadership not only encourages participation but actively nurtures the growth of leaders from all walks of life. This means empowering women to step into leadership roles, not as tokens, but as architects of change. It means fostering an environment where minority voices are not only heard but celebrated for the unique perspectives they offer.

But inclusivity goes beyond representation; it's about creating a culture of respect and empathy. It's about leaders who actively listen, who seek to understand, and who champion the causes of those who might otherwise go unnoticed. It's about a commitment to justice and equality, where the dreams and aspirations of every Sudanese individual are acknowledged and uplifted.

## Education as a Catalyst for Leadership

In the journey towards progress, education becomes a cornerstone. It's not just a means to acquire knowledge; it's a catalyst for leadership. A well-educated population doesn't just enrich the nation's intellectual capital; it empowers individuals to become leaders who drive positive change.

Education instills critical thinking, empowering individuals to question norms and envision alternatives. It equips them with the ability to analyze complex issues, recognize patterns, and develop innovative solutions. Through education, future leaders cultivate a deep understanding of the challenges facing Sudan and the world, preparing them to navigate the intricacies of leadership.

But education is not just about theoretical knowledge; it's about practical skills that empower individuals to be proactive contributors to society. By promoting practical learning, vocational training, and entrepreneurship education, Sudan fosters a generation of leaders who can translate ideas into action, transforming our nation's potential into tangible progress.

Furthermore, education kindles the flame of curiosity and encourages continuous learning. In a rapidly changing world, leaders must be adaptable and open to new ideas. Education provides the foundation for this adaptability, enabling leaders to stay current with advancements in technology, science, and global affairs.

Investment in education, particularly in underserved areas, levels the playing field and ensures that every Sudanese individual has the opportunity to cultivate leadership qualities. It bridges the gap between urban and rural areas, between different socioeconomic backgrounds, and paves the way for leaders to emerge from all corners of the nation.

As Sudan invests in its educational system, it invests in a brighter future, where every educated citizen becomes a potential leader, shaping the destiny of our nation.

## Ethical Leadership and Good Governance

At the heart of visionary leadership lies an unwavering commitment to ethics and good governance. These principles aren't just ideals to strive for; they form the bedrock of a nation's progress and stability. Ethical leaders recognize that their actions are a reflection of their character and values, setting the tone for the entire nation.

Good governance isn't a mere administrative function; it's a promise to uphold transparency, accountability, and the rule of law. It's about leaders who are stewards of public resources, using them for the betterment of the nation rather than personal gain. By establishing strong governance structures, visionary leaders ensure that the nation's potential isn't squandered but channeled towards collective growth.

Ethical leadership extends beyond legality; it's about making decisions that align with the best interests of the Sudanese people. These leaders lead by example, showing through their actions that integrity isn't just a buzzword; it's a guiding principle that informs every decision, no matter how challenging.

An ethical leader's commitment to the people extends to addressing injustices and inequality. By championing social justice, visionary leaders work towards a society where every Sudanese individual has access to basic necessities, opportunities, and the chance to fulfill their potential. This dedication to justice ensures that the progress we achieve is sustainable and inclusive.

## Collaboration and Diplomacy on the Global Stage

As Sudan charts its path to progress, it does not exist in isolation. Global interconnectedness calls for a diplomatic approach that fosters collaboration and engagement on the international stage. Visionary leadership recognizes that our nation's success is intertwined with the global community, and strategic diplomacy is a key to harnessing this interdependence.

Collaboration doesn't just extend to neighboring nations; it encompasses a broad spectrum of global partnerships. By forging alliances with diverse countries, Sudan opens doors to trade, knowledge exchange, and technological advancement. These collaborations allow Sudan to tap into resources that contribute to its development journey.

Diplomacy becomes a tool not just for conflict resolution, but for proactive engagement on issues of regional and global significance. Visionary leaders leverage diplomatic channels to advocate for Sudan's interests, from economic growth to environmental sustainability. Through open dialogue, they build bridges and create opportunities for shared progress.

Sudan's diplomatic efforts go beyond transactional exchanges; they're rooted in a commitment to peace and stability. By fostering mutual understanding and cooperation, visionary leaders contribute to a world where conflicts are resolved through dialogue rather than violence. This diplomatic approach showcases Sudan's commitment to global harmony and reinforces its position as a responsible member of the international community.

## The Future of Leadership in Sudan

As the sun sets on the horizon of possibility, the future of Sudan's leadership unfolds like a canvas waiting to be painted. We stand at the crossroads of history, where the dreams we've cultivated and the ideals we've embraced come to life. The future of Sudan's leadership isn't just a distant mirage; it's a reality we shape through our actions today.

This future is one where the legacy of visionary leadership extends beyond individual leaders and becomes ingrained in the fabric of our society. It's a leadership that doesn't rely on the charisma of a few, but on the collective wisdom and aspirations of the many. Sudan's leadership landscape becomes a mosaic of voices, each contributing a unique hue to the broader picture of progress.

In this future, the youth become torchbearers of transformation. Empowered by education and guided by mentorship, they step onto the stage with boundless energy and fresh perspectives. Their idealism is tempered with practicality, as they navigate the challenges of the modern world armed with the values of inclusivity, ethics, and diplomacy.

The seeds of inclusivity sown today bear fruit, as leaders from diverse backgrounds rise to prominence. Women's voices resonate in corridors of power, shaping policies that reflect the realities of their lived experiences. Marginalized communities find their place at the decision-making table, ensuring that policies are equitable and representative of every Sudanese individual.

Ethical leadership becomes the cornerstone of governance, creating a culture of transparency and accountability that spans generations. The trust forged between leaders and citizens becomes the driving force behind progress, as the Sudanese people are confident that their aspirations are being championed by leaders who prioritize the nation's well-being over personal gain.

On the global stage, Sudan's leadership continues to foster collaboration and diplomacy. The nation's voice is respected and sought after, not just for its resources, but for its ideas and its commitment to peace. Sudan's diplomatic efforts contribute to regional stability, paving the way for economic growth and harmonious coexistence with neighboring nations.

In the future of Sudan's leadership, the lessons of history become the guiding stars that prevent the repetition of past mistakes. Every challenge becomes an opportunity for growth, every setback a lesson in resilience. The legacy of visionary leadership endures, as its impact reverberates through time, inspiring future generations to carry the torch of progress even further.

It's a reality that we have the power to shape through our choices, our actions, and our unwavering commitment to the ideals of progress, unity, and prosperity. The canvas awaits our brushstrokes, and the masterpiece we create will be a testament to the boundless potential of Sudan's visionary leadership.

As we close the chapter on visionary leadership, we stand on the cusp of a future where the dreams we've woven into words become the reality we inhabit. Our journey through the principles of visionary leadership has illuminated the path ahead, guiding us towards a Sudan that is united, prosperous, and a beacon of progress.

The tapestry of leadership that we've explored isn't confined to the pages of this book; it's a living narrative that every Sudanese individual has the power to contribute to. From the nurturing of homegrown leaders to the embrace of inclusivity and the pursuit of ethical governance, each thread we weave adds to the brilliance of our nation's fabric.

Our future is one where Sudan's children grow up with the knowledge that they are the architects of their destiny. They inherit a legacy of visionary leadership that stretches back in time, a legacy that calls them to embody the ideals of progress, empathy, and collaboration. Our youth are our compass, steering us towards uncharted territories of innovation and growth.

The journey of Sudan's leadership doesn't just extend to our borders; it encompasses the globe. Through diplomacy and collaboration, we contribute to a world where unity and understanding triumph over division. Our voice is heard not just for its resonance, but for its commitment to peace and justice.

In the symphony of Sudan's progress, every citizen plays a unique note, a note that harmonizes with the aspirations of fellow Sudanese individuals. Whether a leader at the forefront or a supporter from the sidelines, we all contribute to the crescendo of progress that resounds throughout our nation.

As we step forward into this future, let us be guided by the words of Mahatma Gandhi: "Be the change that you wish to see in the world." Our journey is not one of mere observation; it's a call to action, an invitation to embody the principles of visionary leadership in our everyday lives. Let us remember that transformation doesn't happen overnight; it's a gradual journey marked by persistence, resilience, and the unwavering belief in the potential of our people.

The future we envision is not a fantasy; it's a reality we are sculpting with every decision, every effort, and every dream. Let us stand united, bound by the vision of a Sudan that rises above challenges, embraces diversity, and paves the way for a brighter tomorrow. As we take these steps, we forge a destiny of greatness, not just for ourselves, but for the generations yet to come.

*"The best way to predict the future is to create it."*

- Abraham Lincoln

# Chapter 7: Policy

In the realm of progress and transformation, the cornerstone lies in visionary policies that breathe life into dreams. Picture a Sudan where the landscape of policy-making is not merely bureaucratic, but a dynamic force propelling the nation towards unity and prosperity. These policies, woven with threads of hope and practicality, are poised to redefine the trajectory of our beloved South Sudan and Sudan.

Education, the bedrock of a thriving society, stands at the forefront of our policy revolution. No longer confined to the traditional confines, it emerges as a beacon of enlightenment, accessible to every eager mind. We foresee a Sudan where learning is not a privilege, but a birthright, where knowledge flows freely, nurturing the minds that will shape our future.

Simultaneously, the canvas of healthcare undergoes a profound transformation. Gone are the days of inaccessible medical facilities; a healthcare renaissance is underway. Quality care is no longer a luxury reserved for the fortunate, but a fundamental right extended to every Sudanese. Preventive measures take precedence, steering us towards a future where wellness is paramount, and ailments are met with swift and compassionate care.

In the realm of economics, we forge a path to prosperity, where opportunities abound for every Sudanese soul. Our policies lay the foundation for a robust economic infrastructure, where innovation thrives and entrepreneurship flourishes. This is not a distant dream but a tangible reality, where the wheels of industry turn in harmony with the aspirations of our people.

Our commitment to environmental stewardship is unwavering. We will talk about sustainability, where the preservation of our natural treasures is a collective endeavor. Renewable resources become the lifeblood of our progress, ensuring that growth is not achieved at the expense of the very earth that sustains us.

Through policies of inclusivity and social equality, we break down barriers that have divided us for far too long. No longer shall the marginalized and the voiceless be relegated to the shadows. Our nation stands tall as a tapestry of diversity, where every thread is celebrated, and every voice is heard. Women, the backbone of our society, rise to positions of authority and influence, their contributions shaping the narrative of our shared future.

Technology, the great equalizer of our age, takes center stage in our policy framework. We embrace the digital revolution, where access to information and connectivity are not luxuries, but fundamental rights. Technological advancements become the driving force behind our progress, propelling us into an era of unprecedented growth and opportunity.

Diplomacy and international relations become the linchpin in our global identity. We extend our hand in friendship, forging alliances with nations near and far. Through collaboration and mutual respect, we position ourselves as a beacon of hope and stability in an ever-changing world.

Security and justice form the bedrock of our society, ensuring that every Sudanese citizen feels safe and protected. Our policies stand as a fortress against threats, safeguarding the aspirations of our people. Justice, fair and unyielding, becomes the cornerstone upon which our society rests, upholding the principles of equality and human rights.

In celebrating our rich cultural tapestry, we rediscover the essence of our identity. Arts, music, and literature become the vibrant expressions of our collective soul, transcending boundaries and unifying us in spirit. Our cultural heritage, a source of immense pride, becomes the unbreakable thread that binds us as one Sudanese family.

We can propelled by policies that breathe life into our collective aspirations. The tapestry of our future unfurls before us, woven with the threads of hope, determination, and unity.

## Educational Empowerment

In the pursuit of a brighter future for Sudan, education emerges as the cornerstone of our endeavors. We envision a renaissance in learning, where classrooms transcend their traditional confines and become vibrant hubs of knowledge and inspiration. Here, education is not a privilege reserved for a select few, but a birthright bestowed upon every eager mind. It is a force that knows no boundaries, reaching the farthest corners of our nation, nurturing the potential that lies within every Sudanese child.

Accessible and inclusive education stands as the bedrock of our vision. No longer will geographical constraints or economic disparities impede the pursuit of knowledge. Our policies strive to dismantle these barriers, ensuring that quality education is within arm's reach of every aspiring student. This is a Sudan where children, regardless of their background, have the tools they need to carve out their own destinies.

The transformation extends beyond the classroom walls. We champion a holistic approach, recognizing that education encompasses not only academics but also the development of character, critical thinking, and creativity. Our students will emerge as well-rounded individuals, equipped to navigate the challenges and opportunities that lie ahead. Through innovative teaching methods and a curriculum attuned to the needs of a rapidly evolving world, we pave the way for a generation of thinkers and doers.

## Healthcare for All

A healthcare revolution is underway, reshaping the landscape of well-being in Sudan. No longer shall access to quality healthcare be a privilege enjoyed by a fortunate few; it is a right extended to every Sudanese citizen. Our policies are the architects of this transformation, laying the groundwork for a system that places the health and well-being of our people at its core.

Preventive care takes precedence, heralding a shift from reactive measures to proactive strategies that keep our citizens in robust health. We invest in community-based programs that empower individuals to take charge of their own wellness, fostering a culture of prevention that ripples across the nation. Regular check-ups, early interventions, and healthy living become the norm, ensuring that ailments are met with swift and effective responses.

Quality medical facilities and skilled healthcare professionals form the backbone of our healthcare system. We invest in the training and development of our medical workforce, equipping them with the expertise and compassion needed to provide world-class care. State-of-the-art hospitals and clinics dot the landscape, serving as beacons of hope and healing for communities far and wide.

In this reimagined healthcare landscape, no one is left behind. We address the unique needs of marginalized communities, ensuring that they have equal access to the care and support they require. Whether in bustling urban centers or remote rural areas, healthcare is a right, not a privilege.

As we forge ahead, our policies are not confined to the present, but they look to the future. Research and innovation become driving forces, propelling Sudan to the forefront of medical advancements. We encourage collaboration between institutions, fostering an environment where breakthroughs are celebrated and shared for the betterment of all.

This is the new face of healthcare in Sudan—a system founded on compassion, accessibility, and excellence. It is a testament to our commitment to the well-being of every Sudanese citizen, a promise that their health and happiness are paramount in our vision for a united and prosperous nation.

**Economic Renaissance**

In the grand tapestry of Sudan's transformation, the economic realm emerges as a vibrant thread, woven with aspirations of prosperity and progress. Our policies lay the foundation for a robust economic infrastructure, where innovation thrives and entrepreneurship flourishes. This is not a distant dream, but a tangible reality, where the wheels of industry turn in harmony with the aspirations of our people.

Central to this economic renaissance is the empowerment of small and medium-sized enterprises (SMEs). We recognize that they form the lifeblood of our economy, driving innovation, creating jobs, and fostering a spirit of entrepreneurship. Through targeted policies that provide access to capital, resources, and market opportunities, we pave the way for a new generation of business leaders to emerge.

Investment in key industries is paramount. We identify sectors with untapped potential, from agriculture to technology, and channel resources towards their growth. By strategically positioning ourselves in the global market, we open doors to new avenues of trade and collaboration, bolstering the resilience of our economy.

Furthermore, we champion financial literacy and inclusion, ensuring that every Sudanese citizen has the knowledge and access to financial services needed to participate fully in our economic resurgence. Through initiatives that promote savings, investment, and responsible financial practices, we equip individuals with the tools to build a secure and prosperous future.

## Environmental Stewardship

The call to safeguard our natural heritage resonates deeply in our vision for a transformed Sudan. Our policies herald a commitment to sustainability, where the preservation of our environment is not a choice, but an imperative. It is a promise to future generations that they will inherit a land teeming with the same beauty and abundance that we cherish today.

Renewable resources take center stage in our pursuit of a sustainable future. We invest in clean energy technologies, harnessing the power of sun, wind, and water to fuel our progress. This shift not only reduces our environmental footprint but also positions Sudan as a global leader in the transition towards a greener, more sustainable world.

Conservation becomes a cornerstone of our environmental policy. We protect and restore vital ecosystems, from lush forests to arid savannas, recognizing their intrinsic value to our nation's biodiversity and well-being. Through responsible land management and wildlife preservation efforts, we ensure that Sudan remains a sanctuary for both nature and humanity.

Community engagement is key in our environmental stewardship journey. We foster a sense of ownership and pride among our citizens, empowering them to actively participate in the protection and restoration of their natural surroundings. Through education, awareness campaigns, and collaborative initiatives, we create a nationwide movement dedicated to the preservation of our shared home.

In this vision of environmental stewardship, prosperity and sustainability are not mutually exclusive. Our policies prove that by nurturing the land that sustains us, we pave the way for a future where Sudan thrives in harmony with nature. It is a promise kept to our children, a testament to our dedication to the land we call home.

## Social Equality and Inclusivity

In the tapestry of our united Sudan, threads of diversity and unity intertwine, creating a vibrant tableau of shared humanity. Our policies are forged with the belief that every Sudanese citizen, regardless of background, deserves equal opportunities and rights. We embark on a journey to break down the barriers that have divided us for far too long.

Women, the backbone of our society, rise to positions of authority and influence, their contributions shaping the narrative of our shared future. Through targeted policies that empower and support women in all facets of life, we foster an environment where their potential knows no bounds. This is a Sudan where gender does not limit opportunity, but rather serves as a source of strength and resilience.

Inclusivity extends beyond gender, encompassing marginalized communities and individuals of all abilities. Our policies champion accessibility, ensuring that every Sudanese citizen has the opportunity to participate fully in our society. Through initiatives that promote education, employment, and social integration, we create a nation where every voice is heard and valued.

Together, we celebrate our diversity as a source of strength, recognizing that it is through our differences that we find our greatest collective potential. Our policies pave the way for a more inclusive and harmonious Sudan, where unity is not a mere aspiration, but a lived reality.

## Technological Advancements

In the narrative of Sudan's transformation, technology emerges as the beacon that illuminates our path to progress. We embrace the digital revolution, where access to information and connectivity are not luxuries, but fundamental rights. Our policies position Sudan at the forefront of technological advancements, propelling us into an era of unprecedented growth and opportunity.

The digital divide becomes a thing of the past. We invest in infrastructure that ensures high-speed internet access reaches every corner of our nation, from bustling urban centers to remote rural communities. This connectivity becomes the lifeblood of our progress, opening doors to education, innovation, and economic empowerment.

Innovation becomes a driving force in our economy. We cultivate a culture of creativity and entrepreneurship, providing support and resources to the visionaries and inventors who will shape our future. Through policies that encourage research and development, we foster an environment where Sudanese ingenuity can thrive.

The transformative power of technology extends beyond borders. Through collaborations and partnerships with the global tech community, we position Sudan as a hub for innovation and a player on the world stage. Our policies not only adapt to the rapid pace of technological change but also anticipate and drive it, ensuring that our nation remains at the forefront of progress.

As we embrace technological advancements, we do so with a vision of inclusivity and accessibility. We ensure that the benefits of technology reach every Sudanese citizen, regardless of age, background, or location. Through digital literacy programs and initiatives that promote digital inclusion, we empower our people to navigate the digital landscape with confidence and skill.

This is the technological renaissance of Sudan—a journey that propels us into a future defined by progress, innovation, and boundless opportunity. Our policies lay the groundwork for a Sudan where technology is not a privilege but a tool for empowerment, a force that shapes the destiny of our united nation.

## Diplomacy and International Relations

In the global arena, Sudan stands poised to take its place as a beacon of hope and stability. Our policies in diplomacy and international relations chart a course towards forging strong bonds with nations near and far. We extend our hand in friendship, recognizing that collaboration and mutual respect are the cornerstones of a peaceful world.

Through strategic alliances and partnerships, we position Sudan as a valued player on the international stage. Our policies seek to build bridges of understanding and cooperation, fostering relationships that transcend political boundaries. By engaging in meaningful dialogue and shared initiatives, we contribute to a world where nations work hand in hand for the betterment of all.

Advocating for peace and stability becomes a central tenet of our foreign policy. We lend our voice to global efforts aimed at conflict resolution and humanitarian assistance. Our policies reflect a commitment to upholding the principles of human rights and social justice, both within our borders and on the world stage.

As Sudan takes its place among the community of nations, we do so with a sense of responsibility and a vision of positive impact. Through our policies in diplomacy and international relations, we seek not only to safeguard our own interests but also to contribute to a world where cooperation and understanding prevail.

**Security and Justice**

A nation's strength lies not only in its physical borders but in the safety and security of its citizens. Our policies in security and justice are anchored in the belief that every Sudanese individual deserves to live free from fear and to have their rights protected.

We invest in a robust security framework that safeguards our nation from internal and external threats. Our policies are designed to equip our security forces with the tools, training, and resources they need to uphold the rule of law and maintain peace. Through intelligence sharing and collaboration with international partners, we fortify our defenses and ensure the safety of our citizens.

Justice, fair and unyielding, becomes the cornerstone upon which our society rests. Our policies are dedicated to creating a legal framework that ensures equal access to justice for all Sudanese citizens. We champion the principles of transparency, accountability, and due process, recognizing that a just society is one where every individual's rights are respected and protected.

In times of crisis or conflict, our policies emphasize conflict resolution and reconciliation. We seek to address the root causes of tensions and disputes, working towards solutions that promote long-lasting peace. Through mediation, dialogue, and community engagement, we foster an environment where grievances are heard and addressed, and where unity prevails.

As we forge ahead in the realm of security and justice, we do so with a vision of a Sudan where every citizen feels safe and protected. Our policies are a testament to our commitment to the well-being and security of our people, a promise that their rights will be upheld and their voices will be heard. In this vision, Sudan stands as a nation where justice prevails, and where every individual can live with dignity and without fear.

**Cultural Renaissance**

In the heart of Sudan's transformation lies a celebration of our rich cultural tapestry. Our policies in this realm aim to rekindle a sense of pride and unity in our shared heritage. We envision a Sudan where cultural diversity is not only acknowledged but celebrated as a source of strength.

Arts, music, and literature emerge as powerful expressions of our collective soul. Our policies support and promote the creative endeavors of our artists, musicians, and writers, recognizing their vital role in shaping our cultural narrative. Through exhibitions, performances, and literary festivals, we provide platforms for our cultural ambassadors to showcase their talents and inspire the nation.

Cultural education becomes a cornerstone of our vision. We instill a sense of cultural appreciation and understanding from an early age, ensuring that future generations carry forward the legacy of our traditions. Our policies support initiatives that preserve and transmit our cultural heritage, from traditional crafts to storytelling, ensuring that they remain vibrant and relevant in a modern world.

By embracing our cultural roots, we strengthen the bonds that unite us as a people. Our policies aim to create spaces for cultural exchange and dialogue, where different communities can come together to learn from one another. Through initiatives that promote intercultural understanding and appreciation, we foster an environment where diversity is celebrated as a source of enrichment for all.

In this cultural renaissance, Sudan rediscovers its identity and proudly showcases the beauty of its traditions to the world. Our policies affirm that our cultural heritage is not a relic of the past, but a living, dynamic force that shapes our present and future. Through this celebration of our shared cultural wealth, Sudan stands tall as a nation where unity is forged through the threads of our diverse tapestry.

## A Unified Sudan, A Brighter Future

As we draw the curtains on this vision for Sudan, we stand at the precipice of a new era. The tapestry of dreams that we've woven together envisions a Sudan where unity, progress, and prosperity reign supreme. This is not merely a vision, but a call to action, an invitation to each Sudanese citizen to play their part in the realization of our collective aspirations.

In this tapestry, every thread represents a policy, a commitment, and a promise to our people. It weaves together the hopes, the talents, and the potential of every Sudanese individual. It is a testament to our belief that when we stand united, there is no limit to what we can achieve.

We will break down barriers, empower the marginalized, and champion the cause of justice. We will celebrate our diversity, preserve our cultural heritage, and propel our nation towards a brighter future. Through education, innovation, and collaboration, we will transform Sudan into a beacon of progress and a source of inspiration for the world.

Let us remember the words of Nelson Mandela, who said, *"It always seems impossible until it is done."* Our vision for Sudan may seem ambitious, but it is within our grasp. With determination, unity, and unwavering belief in our potential, we will turn this vision into reality.

We must usher in a new dawn for Sudan, a future where every Sudanese citizen can stand tall with pride, knowing that they have played a part in the transformation of our beloved nation. Sudan will build a legacy of unity, progress, and prosperity that will inspire generations to come.

In the words of Mahatma Gandhi, "*You must be the change you want to see in the world.*" Let us be that change, let us be the architects of our own destiny. The future of Sudan is in our hands, and together, we will write a story of triumph, resilience, and unity that will echo through the ages.

# Chapter 8: Female Empowerment

*Breaking the Mold: A Harmonious Path to Female Empowerment*

Imagine a world where the symphony of human existence plays not just in harmony but in perfect unity, where every note, every instrument, and every performer matters equally. A world where gender doesn't define destiny, but rather, humanity's shared aspirations and dreams unite us all.

Through the landscapes of female empowerment, guided by the wisdom born from straddling two worlds - South Sudan and Canada. Here, we challenge the status quo and reshape the narrative, forging a new path towards empowerment.

Much like a skilled conductor weaving together the diverse melodies of an orchestra, we will explore the intricacies of gender equality by acknowledging the unique strengths of both men and women. Just as a symphony is not complete without every instrument playing its part, humanity thrives when we all embrace our roles in fostering respect, understanding, care, and love.

To set the stage for this transformative journey, let's consider a vivid analogy: the puzzle. Picture a jigsaw puzzle, each piece representing a different facet of society. For centuries, some pieces have been deemed less important, less valuable, or even missing altogether. In this chapter, we aim to locate those missing pieces, to complete the puzzle and reveal the awe-inspiring picture of a world where both women and men stand on equal footing.

But this isn't just about fixing a puzzle; it's about breaking the mold that has confined us for too long. It's about recognizing the profound power of feminine influence and collaboration, not only as a means of progress but as the driving force behind our shared destiny. Just as a sculptor refines a rough stone into a masterpiece, we will explore the potential for growth, development, and unity when we chip away at outdated beliefs and societal norms.

Join us as we journey through the chapters ahead, delving into the challenges faced by women and the solutions that lead to a more harmonious and empowered world. Together, we will venture into the heart of humanity, where the cadence of cooperation and the melody of equality form the backdrop for a brighter future.

Welcome to a world where breaking the mold is the symphony we all play, where anything is possible when we unite in pursuit of a more equitable world.

## Overcoming Historical Challenges

In the grand tapestry of human history, women's voices have often been muted, their potential restrained by the weight of societal norms and cultural biases. Like a shadow that stretches across the centuries, discrimination has cast a pall over opportunities and dreams. It has been a pervasive force, limiting the scope of what women can achieve. Yet, within this darkness, a spark of resilience has always ignited.

Throughout the ages, women have risen above adversity with a determination that is nothing short of awe-inspiring. From suffragettes fighting for the right to vote to pioneers in male-dominated fields, their courage and tenacity have cut through the oppressive fog. They have shattered glass ceilings, proving time and again that limitations imposed by society are merely illusions waiting to be dispelled.

The journey towards cosmic balance for women is not a straightforward, well-paved road. It is a winding path, marked by bumps and bends, where progress is measured not in miles but in collective awakening. It is a journey that necessitates understanding, empathy, and collective action. Breaking free from the chains of historical oppression requires a united front, one that acknowledges the strength and significance of each individual's contribution, regardless of gender.

As we reflect on the struggles of the past, we must also recognize the progress that has been made. Laws have changed, societies have evolved, and opportunities have expanded. Yet, the echoes of history still reverberate in the present, reminding us that there is much work to be done. The stories of women who have paved the way serve as beacons of hope and inspiration, urging us to continue the fight for equality.

## The Importance of Conscious Coexistence

In the intricate tapestry of life, companionship and collaboration are the threads that bind us all. Beyond the confines of matrimony, lies a vast expanse of opportunities for mutual understanding and teamwork. It is in these moments of shared purpose that the true potential of humanity shines brightest. Like two feet propelling us forward, men and women are not in competition, but in concert, each playing an indispensable role in the symphony of progress.

In this interconnected world, recognizing the unique strengths and perspectives that each gender brings to the table is essential. It is not a matter of superiority, but of synergy; a recognition that together, we create a force that is greater than the sum of its parts. Men and women complement one another, each contributing their unique gifts to the collective journey of humanity.

Companionship is not solely about romantic relationships, but about the bonds we form with friends, family, colleagues, and even strangers. It is about recognizing that every individual, regardless of gender, has something valuable to offer. In these connections, we find the power to forge a future where equality isn't a distant goal, but a lived reality.

Through conscious coexistence, we discover the limitless potential that emerges when we stand hand in hand, committed to a shared vision of progress. It is a recognition that together, we are stronger, and that the truest measure of success is not in personal achievement, but in the collective upliftment of all. In embracing conscious coexistence, we embrace the boundless possibilities that await when we come together in unity and purpose.

## Exchanging Efforts: Female Empowerment in Action

In the grand narrative of progress, it is imperative that we recognize the tremendous potential that lies within the power of female emotional influence. This force, often underestimated and overlooked, possesses the capacity to reshape societies, dismantle oppressive systems, and forge new paths towards equality. It is not a call for a replacement of one dominant force with another, but an invitation to integrate a more balanced approach, where the compassionate and nurturing qualities inherent in women are given their due weight in decision-making and leadership.

The outdated paradigms of control and dominance that have defined much of history must yield to the creative and empathetic touch of female empowerment. The world does not suffer from an abundance of compassion; rather, it hungers for it. By tapping into this wellspring of emotional intelligence, we unlock new solutions to age-old problems.

This is not a mere philosophical endeavor; it is a practical necessity in a world grappling with complex challenges that demand nuanced approaches.

In this endeavor, women are not seeking power for its own sake, but rather the opportunity to contribute their unique perspective, informed by the depth of their emotional experiences. It is a call for a more inclusive and holistic decision-making process, where empathy is not a weakness, but a strength. It is a recognition that true progress is not achieved by the exertion of control, but by the cultivation of understanding and cooperation.

## Empowerment through Forgiveness and Self-Correction

Forgiveness is a beacon of light that illuminates the path towards healing and transformation. It is not an act of weakness, but a demonstration of immense strength. When women find the courage to forgive, not in a bid to forget, but as an act of self-liberation and reclamation of agency, they break free from the chains that once bound them. It is a declaration that the cycle of abuse and oppression ends with them.

It is crucial to distinguish between forgiveness that perpetuates a cycle of victimization and forgiveness that empowers. The latter is an act of profound self-love and self-correction. It is a conscious choice to release the burdens of the past, not as a means of condoning the actions of the oppressor, but as a declaration that the power to shape one's destiny lies within. It is a refusal to be defined by past traumas, but a commitment to rise above them.

Self-correction is not an admission of fault, but an acknowledgment of agency. It is a recognition that one possesses the power to redirect their narrative, to transcend the limitations that have been imposed upon them. It is a reclaiming of one's autonomy, a declaration that the course of one's life is determined by one's own choices, not the actions of others.

In this journey towards empowerment through forgiveness and self-correction, women emerge not as victims, but as victors. They become architects of their own destinies, wielding the power to shape a future that is not bound by the shadows of the past. It is a journey of self-discovery, a testament to the resilience and strength that lie within every woman. Through forgiveness and self-correction, women not only heal themselves but become beacons of hope and inspiration for others seeking their own path to empowerment.

## Equitable Access: Resources and Opportunities

In the pursuit of female empowerment, it is imperative that we address the imbalances that persist in access to resources and opportunities. The materialistic resources and job opportunities that drive progress and prosperity are not rare commodities; rather, they are abundant and diverse. However, the distribution of these resources has often been skewed, leaving women at a disadvantage. It is not a question of scarcity, but of equitable distribution.

The reluctance to share the circle of life, to extend a hand of opportunity to all, perpetuates a cycle of inequality. It is a cycle that stifles potential, limiting the contributions of half of the population. When women are denied access to education, economic opportunities, and resources, it is not only a disservice to them, but to society as a whole. It is akin to planting a garden and withholding water from half of the seeds, expecting the entire garden to flourish.

Addressing these disparities requires a collective commitment to dismantling the barriers that hinder access. It necessitates a shift in mindset, from viewing resources as finite and exclusive, to recognizing their potential to fuel the collective progress of society. It is a call to action for governments, institutions, and individuals to invest in the empowerment of women, not as a charitable act, but as an investment in a more prosperous and harmonious future.

Empowering women with equal access to resources and opportunities is not about charity; it is about justice. It is about recognizing the inherent worth and potential of every individual, regardless of their gender. It is a recognition that progress is not a zero-sum game, but a shared journey towards a brighter future.

# The Evolutionary Success of Female Empowerment

The true measure of success in the journey towards female empowerment is not in reaching the top, but in setting an example of leadership that begins with oneself. It is about recognizing that empowerment is not a destination, but a continuous process of growth, self-discovery, and contribution to society. It is a journey that begins with personal agency and extends to the empowerment of others.

Providing women with the tools for success is not about handing them a blueprint, but about equipping them with the skills, knowledge, and confidence to forge their own paths. It is about fostering an environment where women are encouraged to take risks, pursue their passions, and challenge the status quo. It is a recognition that true empowerment lies not in conformity, but in the freedom to be authentically oneself.

Education, worldly experience, and traditional knowledge and wisdom are the cornerstones of this journey. They provide women with the foundation upon which they can build their dreams and aspirations. They open doors to new possibilities, allowing women to explore their potential and contribute meaningfully to society.

The evolution of female empowerment is not a solitary endeavor, but a collective movement that requires the support and participation of all members of society. It is about recognizing that when women thrive, society thrives. It is a call to action for individuals, communities, and institutions to champion the cause of female empowerment, not as a token gesture, but as a fundamental principle of a just and equitable society.

In this journey, women do not seek to replace one dominant force with another, but to create a balanced and inclusive paradigm where the strengths of all individuals, regardless of gender, are celebrated and harnessed for the betterment of society. It is a vision of a world where empowerment is not an exception, but a norm. It is a call to embrace the infinite potential that emerges when we uplift and empower women to be architects of their own destinies.

As we conclude this exploration of female empowerment, we stand at the threshold of a new era—a time when the echoes of history mingle with the promise of a brighter future. The journey we've undertaken together has been a testament to the resilience, strength, and potential of women around the world. It is a journey marked by the recognition that true progress is not a solitary endeavor, but a collective movement towards a more equitable and just society.

In this quest for empowerment, we have uncovered the transformative power of female emotional influence, challenging outdated paradigms and calling for a more balanced approach to decision-making and leadership. We have delved into the liberating force of forgiveness and self-correction, witnessing the triumph of the human spirit over adversity. We have examined the critical need for equitable access to resources and opportunities, recognizing that true empowerment begins with a level playing field.

As we look ahead, it is clear that the evolution of female empowerment is not a finite goal, but an ongoing journey of growth and self-discovery. It is a journey that requires the active participation and support of all members of society. It is a call to action for individuals, communities, and institutions to champion the cause of empowerment, not as a token gesture, but as a fundamental principle of a just and equitable world.

In the words of Eleanor Roosevelt, *"The future belongs to those who believe in the beauty of their dreams."* It is a reminder that the dreams and aspirations of women are not mere fantasies, but the seeds of a future where equality, respect, and understanding flourish. It is a future where the potential of every individual, regardless of gender, is nurtured and celebrated.

As we move forward, let us carry with us the wisdom of Maya Angelou, who said, *"Each time a woman stands up for herself, without knowing it possibly, without claiming it, she stands up for all women."* Let us remember that every step towards empowerment is a step towards a more inclusive and just society, benefiting not only women, but the entire human family.

In closing, let us embrace the infinite potential that emerges when we uplift and empower women to be architects of their own destinies. For in doing so, we shape a future where anything is possible, where the symphony of humanity plays in perfect harmony, and where the collective dreams of women and men unite to create a world that is truly worthy of all.

# Chapter 9: Youth

In revisiting the overarching theme of hope, progress, and transformation for Sudan (Ofiyok), we embark on a poignant journey that encapsulates the very essence of the nation's aspirations. This chapter serves as a reflective canvas, painting a narrative of resilience, determination, and the unwavering spirit of a people destined for greatness.

Against the backdrop of Sudan's historical challenges, the lens now focuses on the beacon of hope that emanates from the hearts and minds of its youth. It is a testament to the enduring spirit that believes in the potential for progress and the transformative power within the grasp of Sudanese (Ofiyok) youth. In acknowledging the trials of the past, this chapter stands as a testament to the unwritten potential of a nation on the brink of rediscovery.

The critical role of the youth takes center stage as we delve into the intricate dynamics of societal evolution. The narrative unfolds not as an isolated tale but as a collective saga, with the youth positioned as the architects of Sudan's destiny. It is an acknowledgment of the pivotal role they play in steering the nation toward an era of unprecedented growth and prosperity.

As the pen begins to trace the contours of this chapter, envision the youth not merely as individuals navigating their own destinies but as a collective force shaping the very fabric of Sudanese society. The tone is one of empowerment, acknowledging the potential within the youth to chart a course that transcends the limitations of the past. It is an ode to their resilience, innovation, and collective vision for a Sudan (Ofiyok) that stands as a testament to the strength of its people.

In this introductory segment, the overarching theme of hope, progress, and transformation is rekindled, and the spotlight is firmly cast upon the youth as the torchbearers of Sudan's future. Through their endeavors, the narrative unfolds, inviting readers to witness the unfolding of a chapter where the resilience and determination of the youth become the driving force behind Sudan's ascent to new heights. Welcome to a chapter where hope is not just a sentiment but a rallying call, echoing through the hearts of Sudanese (Ofiyok) youth, guiding the nation towards a future defined by progress and transformation.

## Understanding the Current Landscape: Navigating Challenges, Embracing Opportunities

Embark on a compelling exploration into the intricate fabric of Sudanese (Ofiyok) youth, where dreams converge with the complexities of reality. In this chapter, we unfurl a panorama of aspirations and challenges, depicting the dynamic landscape that shapes the future of Sudan's resilient youth.

Begin by delving into the diverse tapestry of Sudanese (Ofiyok) youth. From the bustling urban centers to the tranquil rural landscapes, each young individual paints a unique portrait of potential. These are stories of dreams, aspirations, and the untapped potential that resides within every Sudanese youth, creating a rich narrative that is both inspiring and reflective of the nation's diverse spirit.

Transition into the realities that cast shadows on the path to progress. In urban and rural landscapes alike, Sudanese (Ofiyok) youth grapple with challenges—educational disparities, economic uncertainties, and societal expectations. These hurdles, though formidable, become the crucible in which the spirit of resilience, determination, and innovation is forged. It is a landscape where challenges are not roadblocks but opportunities for growth.

Amidst challenges, a silver lining emerges. Explore the initiatives and opportunities that await the youth of Sudan (Ofiyok). From grassroots movements to national programs, witness the dawn of a new era where the youth become architects of their destinies. These opportunities, be they in education, employment, or societal integration, act as catalysts for change, heralding a future where Sudanese (Ofiyok) youth seize the opportunities before them to redefine the narrative of their nation.

In this chapter, the canvas of Sudanese (Ofiyok) youth unfolds, a mosaic painted with the hues of dreams and the intricate patterns of challenges. As we navigate through their stories, envision a landscape where the resilience of the youth becomes the driving force, propelling Sudan toward unprecedented heights of success. Welcome to a chapter where dreams and realities converge, creating a tapestry that reflects the indomitable spirit of Sudanese (Ofiyok) youth in their journey towards a brighter tomorrow.

## Education as the Cornerstone: Illuminating Minds, Empowering Futures

In the heart of Sudanese (Ofiyok) youth lies the transformative power of education, a luminescent force that not only imparts knowledge but acts as a guiding light toward a future brimming with promise. Within the pages of this section, we navigate through the landscape of education, recognizing its pivotal role in shaping the destinies of the youth.

Delving into the intricacies of the current state of education, we uncover both its triumphs and challenges. From urban centers to the far reaches of rural landscapes, education stands as a beacon of hope, offering pathways to enlightenment. However, alongside its successes, there exist urgent needs for reform—disparities in accessibility, varying levels of quality, and the demand for a curriculum that resonates with the contemporary needs of the youth.

As we journey deeper, we encounter initiatives aimed at bridging educational gaps and fostering inclusivity. The very essence of education lies in its ability to transcend boundaries, providing equal opportunities for growth regardless of geographical constraints. In classrooms, both physical and virtual, the youth are equipped with the tools not only to grasp knowledge but to wield it as a force for collective empowerment.

Technology, the harbinger of change in the 21st century, becomes an integral part of this educational odyssey. The infusion of cutting-edge technology into classrooms propels education beyond traditional boundaries. STEM education, with its emphasis on science, technology, engineering, and mathematics, emerges as a conduit for unleashing the innovative potential within young minds. The classroom of tomorrow is not confined to four walls; it is a dynamic space where technology dismantles barriers and opens gateways to knowledge for all.

Yet, education is more than an accumulation of facts; it is a transformative journey from learners to leaders. Initiatives within Sudan (Ofiyok) nurture leadership skills, instilling in the youth the confidence to guide the nation toward progress and prosperity. As educational reforms unfold, the vision becomes clear: an educated youth, equipped not only with knowledge but also with the leadership acumen to steer Sudan into unprecedented heights of success.

In this narrative, education emerges as the cornerstone, illuminating minds and empowering futures. It transcends the confines of classrooms, becoming a force that shapes not only the individual but the collective destiny of a nation. As we immerse ourselves in the unfolding stories of educational transformation, envision a Sudan where every young mind is a beacon of knowledge, collectively driving the nation toward a future defined by enlightenment, progress, and unprecedented success. Welcome to the realm where education becomes the catalyst for a generation of empowered and visionary leaders in Sudan (Ofiyok).

## Youth Empowerment Programs

In delving into the realm of youth empowerment programs, the narrative unfolds as a journey through innovative initiatives designed to uplift Sudanese (Ofiyok) youth both economically and socially. These programs represent a collective effort to harness the untapped potential within the younger generation and pave the way for a future marked by progress and self-determination.

One facet of these empowerment initiatives is centered around skill development. Recognizing that skills are the currency of the future, various programs have been introduced to equip the youth with practical abilities that extend beyond the realms of traditional education. Through vocational training, apprenticeships, and hands-on experiences, these initiatives aim to sculpt a generation adept at navigating the complexities of the contemporary world.

Entrepreneurship stands as another pillar within these empowerment programs, fostering a spirit of innovation and self-sufficiency among the youth. By providing resources, mentorship, and avenues for aspiring entrepreneurs to bring their ideas to fruition, these programs seek to cultivate a generation of self-starters who contribute not only to their personal growth but also to the economic vibrancy of Sudan (Ofiyok) at large.

Simultaneously, leadership training emerges as a pivotal component, recognizing that empowerment extends beyond individual accomplishments to collective influence. Youth are guided through mentorship programs, workshops, and immersive experiences that instill the qualities of resilience, vision, and effective communication. The intention is to nurture a cohort of leaders who will play instrumental roles in shaping the socio-economic landscape of Sudan.

The heartbeat of this narrative lies in the stories of young individuals who have not only participated in these programs but have transcended challenges and made significant contributions to society. These success stories serve as beacons, illuminating the transformative power of empowerment initiatives. Through their tales of perseverance, innovation, and societal impact, these individuals become living testaments to the potential unleashed when the youth are given the tools and opportunities to thrive.

In weaving through the fabric of youth empowerment programs, this chapter encapsulates a collective effort to break down barriers, opening doors for the younger generation to flourish economically and socially. It becomes a narrative of transformation, where the youth, armed with skills, entrepreneurship acumen, and leadership qualities, redefine their trajectories. The success stories within this chapter are not just anecdotes; they are living proof that empowerment programs are catalysts for change, propelling Sudanese (Ofiyok) youth into positions where they become architects of their destinies and contributors to the broader narrative of national progress.

## Cultural Identity and Pride

Venturing into the exploration of cultural identity and pride, the narrative unfurls as a tapestry woven with the rich threads of Sudanese (Ofiyok) heritage. It delves into the collective consciousness of the youth, exploring the significance of preserving and celebrating cultural roots in a landscape undergoing transformation.

Amidst the challenges of the contemporary world, there's a concerted effort to embed cultural education into the very fabric of Sudanese society. It is an acknowledgment that amidst progress, the cultural identity of a nation should stand tall, a beacon that guides the youth in navigating the complexities of the modern era. By integrating cultural education into mainstream schooling, initiatives aim to ensure that the younger generation remains deeply connected to its roots.

Beyond the confines of classrooms, cultural exchange programs emerge as bridges connecting diverse segments of Sudanese (Ofiyok) society. These programs create spaces where the youth from different backgrounds converge, fostering a sense of unity and shared identity. It's not just about preserving cultural heritage but also about weaving a collective narrative that binds the youth together, irrespective of their diverse backgrounds.

The role of cultural identity in nurturing a sense of pride becomes evident in the stories of individuals who actively participate in cultural initiatives. These narratives echo the sentiment that cultural pride is not a vestige of the past but a living, breathing force that influences how the youth perceive themselves and their place in Sudanese (Ofiyok) society.

In exploring the realm of cultural identity and pride, this chapter embodies a commitment to recognizing the value of heritage in the midst of societal transformation. It envisions a Sudan where the youth, deeply rooted in their cultural identities, become not only bearers of tradition but active participants in shaping a collective future. The narrative transcends the dichotomy of tradition and progress, painting a picture of Sudanese (Ofiyok) youth who, with cultural pride as their compass, navigate the evolving landscape with a sense of purpose and belonging.

## Gender Equality and Women Empowerment

Within the narrative of Sudanese (Ofiyok) transformation, the exploration of gender equality and women's empowerment takes center stage. It unfolds as a story of breaking barriers, challenging societal norms, and fostering a landscape where the potential of women is not just recognized but actively nurtured.

Efforts to break down gender barriers extend across education, employment, and leadership roles. Initiatives strive to create an inclusive environment, ensuring that young women have equal access to educational opportunities. This isn't merely about imparting knowledge but about empowering women with the tools they need to become architects of their destinies. The chapters of this narrative transcend into the professional realm, where women are encouraged and supported to pursue careers and leadership positions traditionally dominated by men.

Stories of inspirational women emerge as beacons, illuminating the transformative power of gender equality and women's empowerment. These narratives aren't just about individual achievements but about reshaping societal expectations. From overcoming obstacles in traditionally male-dominated fields to spearheading social initiatives, these women redefine what is possible for Sudanese (Ofiyok) women, inspiring future generations to aspire beyond imposed limitations.

## Environmental Stewardship

In the evolving narrative of Sudanese (Ofiyok) progress, the chapter on environmental stewardship emerges as a call to action, urging the youth to become guardians of their natural heritage. It paints a picture of a nation where the younger generation not only recognizes the intrinsic value of their environment but actively engages in preserving it for future generations.

Environmental education becomes a cornerstone, instilling in the youth an understanding of their role as custodians of the Earth. Beyond knowledge, initiatives focus on practical steps, encouraging sustainable practices, conservation efforts, and responsible resource management. The youth are not just observers but active participants in initiatives that address climate change and environmental challenges.

The narrative extends into stories of young individuals who have taken up the mantle of environmental stewardship. From community-based conservation projects to advocating for sustainable practices in urban settings, these stories become testaments to the transformative impact of youth-driven environmental initiatives. It's about recognizing the interconnectedness of humanity and nature, fostering a sense of responsibility that goes beyond individual actions.

As we traverse through the chapters on gender equality and environmental stewardship, the narrative takes on a multidimensional hue. It becomes a story of inclusivity, where the empowerment of women and the protection of the environment are not separate endeavors but interconnected facets of Sudanese (Ofiyok) progress. These chapters invite readers to envision a nation where gender equality is not a distant goal but a lived reality, and environmental stewardship is a collective ethos that shapes the very fabric of Sudanese society.

## Technological Advancements and Innovation

In the unfolding narrative of Sudanese (Ofiyok) progress, the chapters on technological advancements and innovation resonate as catalysts propelling the nation into a future defined by connectivity, creativity, and unprecedented possibilities. The youth, as torchbearers of change, find themselves at the forefront of this transformative journey.

Technological advancements are not merely embraced for the sake of progress but are integrated into the very fabric of education, reshaping how the youth learn and engage with the world. Digital literacy becomes a cornerstone, ensuring that the younger generation is not only equipped with traditional knowledge but is also adept at navigating the evolving landscape of technology.

Beyond education, the narrative extends into the realm of innovation, where the youth are encouraged to think outside the conventional boundaries. Entrepreneurial ecosystems thrive, providing platforms for young minds to incubate and materialize groundbreaking ideas. The narrative weaves through stories of startups, tech innovations, and young minds contributing to Sudan's (Ofiyok) technological tapestry.

## Global Collaborations and Diplomacy

As the narrative reaches the chapter on global collaborations and diplomacy, Sudanese (Ofiyok) youth find themselves not only as architects of national progress but as ambassadors on the global stage. The emphasis is on fostering relationships beyond borders, leveraging international partnerships to enrich the nation's cultural, economic, and technological landscape.

Educational exchange programs become conduits for fostering global understanding, allowing Sudanese youth to experience different cultures and perspectives firsthand. These initiatives not only contribute to individual growth but also position the youth as ambassadors who bridge cultural gaps and build international connections.

The realm of diplomacy is no longer confined to government corridors but extends to the grassroots level, where young individuals actively engage in initiatives that foster international cooperation. From cultural exchange events to collaborative projects addressing global challenges, Sudanese (Ofiyok) youth step into roles that transcend national boundaries, contributing to a narrative where global collaborations are integral to Sudan's journey of progress and transformation.

In the interconnected chapters of technological advancements, innovation, global collaborations, and diplomacy, the narrative transcends the confines of national borders. Sudanese (Ofiyok) youth, equipped with technological prowess and a global perspective, become key players in shaping not only the destiny of their nation but also contributing to the larger narrative of a harmonious, interconnected global community. These chapters symbolize a Sudan that is not isolated but actively participating in the global dialogue of progress and cooperation.

## The Road Ahead: A Vision Unveiled

As we tread the concluding steps of this narrative, we stand at the intersection of dreams and realities, where the road ahead for Sudanese (Ofiyok) is illuminated by the collective efforts of a dynamic and determined youth. The journey we've undertaken together through the chapters of hope, progress, and transformation unveils a vision that extends beyond the horizon, promising a future defined by resilience, innovation, and unity.

In the tapestry of Sudan's future, the role of the youth emerges not merely as a demographic but as the driving force propelling the nation toward unprecedented heights. From cultural preservation to technological innovation, gender equality to environmental stewardship, Sudanese (Ofiyok) youth stand as architects shaping a narrative that reflects the values, aspirations, and collective spirit of a nation on the cusp of a transformative era.

The pages of this chapter have unfolded stories of triumphs over challenges, of resilience in the face of adversity, and of a relentless pursuit of progress. It paints a vivid picture of a Sudanese (Ofiyok) society where every young mind is nurtured, every voice is heard, and every dream is encouraged to take flight.

As we gaze toward the road ahead, let this vision serve as a guiding light, a compass directing the youth toward endeavors that transcend individual pursuits and contribute to the collective tapestry of Sudanese (Ofiyok) progress. The challenges that lie ahead are not insurmountable but rather stepping stones toward greater heights of achievement and unity.

In the words of Nelson Mandela, "It always seems impossible until it's done." The road ahead for Sudanese (Ofiyok) is a journey that may seem daunting at times, but through collective determination, unwavering hope, and the boundless potential of the youth, every aspiration woven into the fabric of this narrative is within reach.

As we conclude this chapter and look forward to the unfolding chapters of Sudan's future, may the spirit of unity, progress, and transformation carry us forward, paving the way for a nation that stands as a testament to the indomitable spirit of its people.

*"The future belongs to those who believe in the beauty of their dreams."*

– Eleanor Roosevelt

# Chapter 10: Healthcare

In the vast tapestry of Sudan's dreams, the landscape of healthcare stands as both a challenge and an untapped reservoir of potential. It is imperative that we examine the existing condition of healthcare critically as we set out on this transforming trip through the corridors of well-being. The canvas is painted with hues of challenges, but within these shadows lie the intricate brushstrokes of opportunities waiting to be unveiled.

Imagine a healthcare system that transcends the conventional, where the pulse of innovation beats in rhythm with the heartbeat of a nation. In the echoes of crowded waiting rooms and the hushed whispers of health-related uncertainties, we find the impetus to redefine what it means to care for the well-being of a people.

We stand at a crossroads, where the vision for healthcare metamorphoses into a beacon of hope, steering away from the conventional narratives. It's a holistic approach, a fusion of traditional wisdom and modern advancements, a symphony where preventive care dances hand in hand with cutting-edge technology.

In this chapter, we navigate the landscape of our aspirations, charting a course toward a healthcare horizon that beckons with promise. We explore the revolutionary potential of technology, imagining a time when telemedicine reaches even the most remote locations, filling the gap that exists between those in need and the care they are entitled to. Yet, this journey is not just about erecting state-of-the-art facilities; it's about dismantling the barriers that stand between communities and quality healthcare. Picture a world where healthcare is not a luxury but a fundamental right, where the pulse of affordable and accessible care resonates across the expanse of the nation.

Our healthcare professionals, the unsung heroes of this narrative, are not just practitioners but torchbearers of change. We invest not only in their education but in a culture that reveres and celebrates their tireless contributions. For it is in empowering those who heal that we pave the way for a healthier, more vibrant Sudan.

We come across the proactive approach of disease prevention and control as we navigate the complexities of this vision. It's a call to action, a pledge to swiftly and precisely combat epidemics as well as to instill a health consciousness in our communities and encourage a shared responsibility for well-being.

Join us in this exploration of collaborative international partnerships, where the expertise of the world converges with the aspirations of Sudan's healthcare renaissance. Together, we envision a future where the borders of healthcare extend far beyond our geographical boundaries.

The chapter ahead is not just about medical charts and prescriptions; it's about recognizing the significance of mental health, embracing sustainable practices, and weaving a narrative that places well-being at the heart of Sudan's progress.

So let us go out into the world of healthcare change, where the stethoscope sounds not just the pulse of a country hoping for a healthier future, but also the rhythm of heartbeats. As we set out on this voyage, the possibilities seem only limited by our daring dreams.

## Vision for Healthcare Transformation

We proceeded on the visionary process of Sudan's healthcare system, going beyond the obvious to tell a story of deep transformation as well as structural reform. This narrative is a symphony of transformation, an enchanting melody heralding a future where the very essence of well-being defies conventional limits.

In this vivid vision, our healthcare system emerges as a tapestry woven with threads of both ancient wisdom and the gleaming filaments of contemporary innovation. It's a marriage of the traditional and the modern, where the age-old practices meet cutting-edge advancements in a dance that defines the very soul of healthcare.

Imagine a society where health is not reduced to the reactive treatment of illnesses but elevated to a culture of preventive care. Picture communities flourishing on the ethos of empowerment, where individuals are equipped with knowledge and tools to proactively safeguard their well-being. This is more than a shift in medical paradigms; it's the cultivation of a resilient nation that thrives on the principles of preventive health maintenance.

At the heart of this transformative journey lies a pulsating rhythm of technological advancements. It's not merely about incorporating digital solutions; it's a comprehensive embrace of telemedicine that transcends convenience to become a vital lifeline. In the remote corners where urban hubs seem like distant mirages, telemedicine emerges as a beacon, ensuring that the right to quality healthcare is not a privilege confined to certain geographies but an inherent right for every Sudanese citizen.

This vision extends beyond the realm of healthcare facilities. It is a commitment to bridge the gaps that have long separated communities from the vital services they deserve. It's a call to establish a healthcare infrastructure that not only symbolizes progress in urban centers but also extends its roots into the very soil of rural villages.

Collaboration becomes the cornerstone, as financial constraints no longer serve as impediments to seeking medical attention. The vision encompasses the establishment of robust financial aid programs, fortified by international partnerships that share our commitment to inclusivity. This is not just a vision for healthcare; it's a blueprint for a more equitable and accessible healthcare landscape that stands as a testament to the collective commitment to the well-being of every Sudanese citizen.

## Accessible and Inclusive Healthcare

As we step into the pragmatic realm of accessible and inclusive healthcare, our vision transcends the confines of the visionary canvas and ventures into the intricate details of implementation. This phase of transformation is not a mere conceptualization; it's the blueprint for a healthcare landscape that intimately touches the lives of every Sudanese citizen.

Imagine a landscape where the presence of healthcare infrastructure is not a distant spectacle reserved for urban centers but a finely woven network that intricately threads through the fabric of every village and town. The vision here is not just about erecting medical facilities; it's about establishing a comprehensive and interconnected system that ensures healthcare is not a privilege dictated by geography but a fundamental right accessible to all.

This inclusivity extends beyond the physical infrastructure to the very heart of financial considerations. The barriers erected by financial constraints shall no longer impede access to medical attention. In this vision, we meticulously explore and implement avenues to render healthcare affordable, breaking down the walls that have for too long hindered individuals from seeking the care they deserve.

As we navigate the intricacies of financial inclusivity, the vision unfolds with the establishment of robust financial aid programs. These programs, fortified by collaborative efforts with international partners, signify a commitment to ensuring that healthcare becomes an attainable reality for everyone, irrespective of economic disparities.

The transformation we strive for is not a distant mirage but a tangible reality, a manifestation of collaboration and unwavering determination. It's about creating a healthcare ecosystem that harmonizes with the pulse of the nation, where the waving flag symbolizes not only political sovereignty but an unyielding commitment to the holistic well-being of every Sudanese citizen.

As collectively, we set out to remove the obstacles preventing accessibility and reinterpret the fundamental principles of inclusivity in healthcare. The goal turns into a call to action, resonating with the shared determination to create a healthier, more vibrant Sudan where healthcare benefits are accessible to all, creating a story of resiliency, prosperity, and unity.

## Empowering Healthcare Professionals

In the pursuit of a reimagined healthcare landscape, the spotlight turns towards the architects of change—the healthcare professionals who are not merely practitioners but torchbearers of a transformed Sudanese health system. This phase of our vision delves into empowering these dedicated individuals, recognizing that their role extends beyond medical expertise to shaping the very core of our nation's well-being.

At the heart of this empowerment lies a commitment to investing in education and training. It's not just about establishing medical schools but creating institutions that stand as crucibles of knowledge, fostering an environment where healthcare professionals are not just practitioners but lifelong learners. Continuous professional development becomes a cornerstone, ensuring that the practitioners of today evolve into the leaders and innovators of tomorrow.

This vision is not only about education but also about valuing and recognizing the tireless contributions of healthcare workers. Compensation packages are not just numbers on a paycheck but a reflection of the societal esteem we place on those who dedicate their lives to healing. Celebrating the contributions of healthcare heroes becomes a cultural norm, fostering an environment where their commitment is not just acknowledged but applauded.

In this phase, we envision a healthcare workforce not bound by limitations but propelled by a sense of purpose and fulfillment. The commitment to excellence goes hand in hand with recognizing that the well-being of the nation is intricately woven into the well-being of its healthcare professionals.

As we empower these professionals, we understand that their impact extends far beyond medical charts and prescriptions. They are the guardians of our collective health, and their empowerment translates into a more robust and responsive healthcare system. This vision is a call to not only uplift the individuals within the healthcare profession but also to elevate the entire nation by recognizing the pivotal role they play in shaping our collective destiny. Together, we forge a path where healthcare professionals are not just practitioners but the architects of a healthier, more vibrant Sudan.

## Innovative Disease Prevention and Control

Venturing deeper into our transformative journey, we focus on the proactive realm of disease prevention and control, where the narrative unfolds beyond the confines of traditional healthcare. In this phase, our vision extends beyond treating ailments to a concerted effort to prevent them, creating a nation that stands resilient against the challenges of health crises.

At the heart of this vision lies a commitment to proactive public health initiatives. Picture a scenario where vaccination programs are not just reactive responses but proactive shields, preventing the outbreak and spread of diseases. It's a commitment to fortify our nation against the threats that lurk on the horizon, ensuring that our communities are shielded from preventable illnesses.

Epidemics, when they arise, become not just challenges but opportunities for swift and effective response strategies. In this vision, the healthcare system is agile, equipped to handle crises with precision and empathy. The response is not just about containment but about fostering a sense of security among the populace, assuring them that their well-being is prioritized.

Yet, the vision transcends the clinical aspects; it delves into community engagement. It's about more than just providing healthcare; it's about creating a societal fabric that actively participates in its well-being. Health awareness campaigns become not just information sessions but communal endeavors where individuals are active participants in their own health journeys.

This phase of the vision is a commitment to not merely reacting to health challenges but actively engaging communities in the pursuit of well-being. It's about fostering a sense of responsibility among individuals to safeguard their health and the health of their communities. The vision here is one where public health is not just a system but a shared responsibility, a collective effort to create a healthier and more resilient Sudan.

As we navigate this phase, we understand that the impact of disease prevention and control extends far beyond the clinical setting. It's a transformative shift in how we perceive and interact with healthcare—a paradigm where the nation actively collaborates to fortify its health, ensuring that every Sudanese citizen is not merely a recipient of healthcare but an active participant in the creation of a healthier and more vibrant Sudan.

## Collaborative International Partnerships

As we turn our gaze outward, recognizing that the journey toward a healthier Sudan is not a solitary endeavor. The vision unfolds in the spirit of collaboration, where international partnerships become the catalysts for change, enriching our healthcare landscape with global expertise and shared commitment.

In this phase, we envision forging alliances with leading healthcare organizations from around the world. These partnerships are not mere transactions but strategic collaborations where knowledge is exchanged, best practices are shared, and innovative solutions are co-created. The vision is to harness the collective wisdom of the global healthcare community to elevate the standards of our own.

Participating in research and development initiatives becomes a cornerstone of this collaborative vision. It's not just about benefiting from global advancements but actively contributing to the collective pool of medical knowledge. Sudan becomes a hub where ideas converge, and breakthroughs are not only welcomed but nurtured to fruition.

This collaborative spirit extends beyond clinical matters; it's a commitment to creating a holistic healthcare ecosystem that transcends borders. The vision here is one of shared responsibility, where the health of Sudanese citizens is not only a national concern but a global priority. International partnerships become a testament to the interconnectedness of our world, where the well-being of one nation contributes to the well-being of all.

As we navigate this phase, we understand that the transformative power of collaboration is not just about the exchange of medical knowledge; it's about fostering a sense of unity and shared purpose. Together, with our international partners, we lay the foundation for a healthcare landscape that is not confined by geographical boundaries but is enriched by the diversity of global perspectives.

## Mental Health and Wellness

Transitioning into a dimension of healthcare often overlooked, our vision extends beyond the physical to the realms of mental health and wellness. This phase of the transformation is an acknowledgment that true well-being is not complete without addressing the intricacies of the mind and soul.

In this vision, mental health is not relegated to the shadows but brought into the spotlight. It's about integrating mental health services seamlessly into primary care, ensuring that the well-being of the mind is as prioritized as that of the body. Stigmas surrounding mental health are dismantled, and seeking support becomes an act of strength and self-care.

The commitment extends to reducing societal stigma through education and advocacy. Mental health awareness becomes not just a campaign but a cultural shift where conversations surrounding mental health are normalized. The vision here is one where individuals feel not only empowered to seek help but also supported by a society that understands and values mental well-being.

As we navigate this phase, we understand that mental health is not a standalone concept but intricately connected to the overall wellness of a nation. It's about creating an environment where the emotional and psychological health of Sudanese citizens is prioritized, fostering a society that recognizes the importance of mental well-being in the pursuit of a healthier and more vibrant Sudan.

## Sustainable Healthcare Practices

In this crucial phase of our healthcare transformation, we turn our attention to sustainability—a vision where the pursuit of well-being harmonizes with the preservation of our environment. Sustainable healthcare practices become not just a necessity but a moral imperative as we navigate the delicate balance between progress and environmental responsibility.

At the core of this vision is a commitment to environmentally conscious healthcare. Picture healthcare facilities that are not just symbols of progress but pioneers of green initiatives. The vision here is to create medical spaces that reduce their ecological footprint, utilizing renewable energy, implementing waste reduction strategies, and embracing sustainable architecture.

The commitment extends to medical research and development, where innovation aligns with environmental stewardship. The vision is to not only advance medical science but to do so in a manner that respects and preserves the natural world. It's about adopting practices that minimize environmental impact and contribute to the collective responsibility of creating a healthier planet.

This phase of the vision recognizes that the health of our citizens is intricately linked to the health of our planet. It's about creating a healthcare system that not only heals individuals but contributes to the broader goal of global sustainability. As we navigate this phase, we understand that the pursuit of well-being should not come at the cost of our environment; rather, the two should complement and reinforce each other in our collective journey towards a healthier, more vibrant Sudan.

## Monitoring and Evaluation

As we progress through the transformative landscape of Sudan's healthcare, the importance of monitoring and evaluation becomes paramount. This phase is not just a checkpoint but an ongoing commitment to ensuring that the envisioned changes are not only implemented but also yielding the intended results.

Establishing performance metrics becomes a cornerstone of this vision. It's about quantifying the impact of healthcare initiatives, tracking outcomes, and measuring the effectiveness of strategies. The vision is to create a system where data is not just collected but utilized to refine and enhance the healthcare landscape continually.

Ensuring accountability and transparency is another pillar of this phase. The vision here is to foster a culture where the healthcare system is not shrouded in mystery but open for scrutiny. Transparency becomes a tool for building trust, and accountability is the linchpin that ensures that the commitment to healthcare transformation remains unwavering.

Navigating this phase is not merely about numbers and statistics; it's about recognizing the dynamic nature of healthcare. It's about flexibility and adaptability, understanding that the path to a healthier Sudan may require course corrections. As we embark on this phase, the vision is clear—to create a healthcare system that is not only transformative but sustains its transformative power through continuous monitoring, evaluation, and a steadfast commitment to the well-being of every Sudanese citizen.

To sum it up, we stand at the intersection of visionary aspirations and tangible actions, witnessing the birth of a redefined healthcare landscape for Sudan. The journey we've undertaken transcends the boundaries of conventional healthcare, painting a picture of a nation where well-being is not just a destination but a continuous, evolving narrative.

Our vision extends beyond the sterile walls of medical facilities; it encompasses the vibrant tapestry of communities actively engaged in their health. Imagine a farmer in a remote village, accessing healthcare through telemedicine, or a young student thriving in a school equipped with the knowledge to prevent illnesses before they strike. These are not mere dreams but the echoes of a future we are actively crafting.

As we dismantle barriers, redefine accessibility, and foster collaborative partnerships, our commitment to healthcare transformation becomes an anthem of resilience. Sudanese citizens are not just recipients of healthcare; they are active participants in the creation of a healthier nation.

In the realm of mental health, we envision a society that values emotional well-being as much as physical health—a society where seeking support for mental health is met with understanding, compassion, and a plethora of resources. It is in this empathetic environment that individuals flourish, contributing to a collective wellness that transcends the confines of clinical care.

Our commitment to sustainability is not a fleeting trend but a profound acknowledgment that the health of our people is intricately linked to the health of our planet. In adopting green initiatives and eco-conscious practices, we forge a path where well-being extends beyond the human realm to encompass the entire ecosystem we call home.

As we close this chapter, the vision becomes a call to action—a call to actively participate in the monitoring and evaluation of our healthcare initiatives. It is in the constant analysis of our efforts that we refine, adapt, and ensure that our healthcare system remains dynamic and responsive to the evolving needs of Sudanese citizens.

In the symphony of healthcare transformation, Sudan is not merely a passive observer but the conductor orchestrating a harmonious melody of well-being. The vision outlined in this chapter is not a static blueprint but a living testament to our collective determination to shape a future where every Sudanese citizen enjoys the benefits of a healthcare system that is inclusive, innovative, and sustainable. The journey continues, and as we navigate through uncharted territories, the heartbeat of a healthier, more vibrant Sudan resonates with each step forward.

# Chapter 11: Infrastructure

In the heart of Sudan's journey towards a renaissance, one cannot help but marvel at the intricacies of its unfolding narrative. As the sun sets over the Nile, casting a golden glow upon the landscape, a vision emerges—one where the veins of progress course through the nation's very foundation. In this chapter, we will look onto a thrilling exploration of Sudan's future, a future anchored in the transformative power of infrastructure.

> *"Infrastructure is not just about roads and buildings; it is the lifeline that breathes vitality into the dreams of a nation."* – Unknown

Imagine standing at the crossroads of history, where every pathway leads to the realization of grand aspirations. The journey begins not merely with bricks and mortar but with the collective heartbeat of a people yearning for a better tomorrow. When we explore Sudan's infrastructure, imagine the sound of development reverberating through vibrant cities, over contemporary roads, and inside cutting-edge establishments.

Picture a vibrant cityscape, illuminated by the glow of streetlights powered by sustainable energy. The hum of electric vehicles gliding silently on well-maintained roads reverberates through the air. In this vision, technology intertwines seamlessly with tradition, creating a tapestry where the past and future coalesce. This is the Sudan we dare to dream—a nation where infrastructure is not just a means to an end but a testament to resilience, determination, and the audacity to dream big.

## Historical Perspective: Foundations of Resilience

Setting off on a voyage through the ages, we explore the rich tapestry of Sudanese history—a story laced with strands of victories and tragedies that shaped the tenacious nation that endures to this day. This historical odyssey unveils the profound evolution of Sudan's infrastructure, a testament to the nation's endurance, adaptation, and unyielding spirit across epochs.

In the annals of time, Sudan's infrastructure narrates a compelling story—a story that begins with ancient trade routes, weaving connections between civilizations and fostering cultural exchange. These routes, like veins carrying the lifeblood of commerce and ideas, laid the groundwork for Sudan's resilience, marking the first strokes on the canvas of its progress.

The historical journey unearths key milestones that echo the tenacity of a people relentlessly striving for progress. The ancient pyramids, standing as architectural marvels, bear witness to the ingenuity of Sudan's forebearers. These monumental structures, etched against the canvas of time, reflect not only engineering prowess but a profound commitment to legacy and cultural richness.

As civilizations ebbed and flowed, Sudan weathered waves of influences—from the vibrant Kingdom of Kush to the challenges brought by external forces. The rise and fall of kingdoms, the spread of Islam, and the encounters with foreign powers all left indelible marks on Sudan's infrastructure. The architectural marvels evolved, incorporating new influences and adapting to changing times.

The medieval cities of Sudan, like Old Dongola and Meroe, stand as silent witnesses to the dynamic interplay of history and resilience. The intricate network of trade routes that once crisscrossed the Sahara became conduits not just for goods but for the exchange of ideas, enriching the cultural mosaic that defines Sudan.

Yet, as we traverse the historical landscape, we encounter chapters marked by challenges—periods of decline and foreign influences that have become integral chapters in the nation's story. The Ottoman and British occupations, each leaving a distinctive mark, tested Sudan's resilience but also became catalysts for newfound strength and unity.

The historical odyssey of Sudan is a mosaic of triumphs and tribulations, a narrative where each challenge met was an opportunity for resilience to flourish. From the ancient trade routes to the challenges of the 21st century, Sudan's history stands as a testament to the enduring spirit that has propelled the nation forward. As we grasp the threads of the past, we gain a deeper appreciation for the foundations of resilience upon which Sudan's contemporary journey is built.

## The Vision for a Modern Sudan: A Tapestry of Progress

Today, against the backdrop of history, we cast our gaze upon the horizon of possibilities—a Sudan envisioned as a beacon of progress. Our aspirations are not confined to mirages but grounded in the tangible transformation of every sector. This is not a mere wish; it is a commitment to sculpt a modern Sudan that seamlessly integrates into the global landscape.

In this vision, roads are not just arteries for transportation but lifelines connecting communities, fostering unity. Energy is not a mere utility; it is a sustainable force propelling industries and illuminating homes. Telecommunications transcend beyond connectivity; they become conduits for innovation and empowerment. Water and sanitation cease to be basic necessities; they evolve into cornerstones of public health and environmental stewardship.

Educational hubs emerge as incubators of brilliance, cultivating minds that challenge the status quo and redefine the nation's destiny. Healthcare becomes a right, not a privilege, as state-of-the-art facilities dot the landscape, ensuring the well-being of every citizen. Smart cities rise, not just as urban marvels, but as testaments to Sudan's technological prowess and commitment to sustainability.

This vision is not a distant mirage but a reality in the making. It's a Sudan where the foundations laid today pave the way for a tomorrow where dreams aren't deferred but embraced. The journey ahead is not without challenges, but the vigor of the Sudanese spirit propels us forward, confident that the ideals we envision will manifest into a Sudan that stands tall on the global stage. Join me as we navigate this transformative landscape, where history meets vision, and infrastructure becomes the bridge to a prosperous future.

## Roads and Transportation: Navigating Connectivity

While exploring of Sudan's visionary future, the transformation of the landscape is nothing short of poetic—a shift from mere geographical features to a complex web of interconnected paths. These pathways are not mere conduits of travel; they are the lifelines that pulse with the commitment to seamless mobility, marking Sudan's steadfast dedication to progress.

In the heart of this transformation, roads cease to be mundane strips of asphalt; they evolve into the beating arteries that propel Sudan's journey forward. No longer confined by city limits, these roads extend their reach, intricately binding urban hubs with the vast expanses of rural terrain. In this interwoven network, diversity thrives, and unity is fostered as these roads become more than just physical connectors—they are symbolic bridges uniting communities and cultures.

But envisioning Sudan's future in transportation goes beyond the traditional scope. The vision extends to incorporate modern transportation systems that redefine the very essence of citizen mobility. Picture electric vehicles seamlessly gliding through urban streets, their noiseless movement echoing not just efficiency but a commitment to reducing the nation's carbon footprint. This forward-thinking approach ushers in an era of sustainability, where progress is harmonized with environmental consciousness.

This commitment to transportation is not a mere logistical promise; it is a pledge to connect not just destinations but the very fabric of Sudanese society—the communities, cultures, and dreams that form the soul of the nation. It ensures that progress is not a privilege confined to specific regions but a promise that resonates in every corner of Sudan.

The roadmap ahead, though ambitious, embodies a profound determination. Each mile signifies more than physical distance covered; it becomes a step toward a nation that is not only accessible but intricately integrated. This journey isn't just about constructing roads; it's about building pathways to prosperity, where every stretch symbolizes the resilience and unwavering determination of the Sudanese people.

In envisaging Sudan's future, the interplay of infrastructure and transportation transcends the physical realm. It becomes a testament to the collective synergy of a united nation, where the barriers of distance are dismantled, and connectivity becomes the cornerstone of progress. The journey unfolds, promising a Sudan where the pathways are not just physical routes but symbolic narratives of a nation propelling itself into an era of unparalleled connectivity and prosperity.

## Energy Revolution: Illuminating Progress

The metamorphosis of the energy landscape unfolds as a profound narrative—a story of transformation from a conventional energy framework to a sustainable force propelling the nation into the future. This narrative isn't just about meeting the immediate energy needs; it's a profound shift, a redefinition of the power dynamics that underpin progress. Sudan envisions a future where energy transcends its role as a mere utility; it becomes a catalyst, a driving force for economic growth, environmental stewardship, and social empowerment.

The vision extends far beyond the confines of conventional energy sources, embracing a revolutionary shift toward renewables that echoes a commitment to a greener, more sustainable future. Picture vast solar fields capturing the sun's energy, their panels glistening under the Sudanese sun. Imagine wind turbines gracefully harnessing the power of the breeze, and hydroelectric plants strategically utilizing Sudan's abundant water resources to generate clean energy. This isn't just a transition; it's a resolute commitment to harnessing the boundless potential of nature for a more sustainable tomorrow.

Sudan's energy revolution is not solely about addressing the demands of today; it's a forward-looking pledge to anticipate and meet the evolving needs of tomorrow. It's a commitment to power industries, illuminate homes, and drive innovation through sustainable means. In this visionary landscape, energy isn't merely a commodity; it transforms into a strategic asset, ensuring the nation's resilience and diminishing reliance on finite resources.

As Sudan lights up its future, it doesn't just illuminate its own path—it becomes a guiding beacon for other nations to follow. This path is one where progress is not fueled by resource depletion but by the boundless energy harnessed from nature. Sudan's energy revolution becomes a beacon, not just for its own commitment to a sustainable future, but for a global community where prosperity harmoniously coexists with environmental consciousness. It's a testament to Sudan's dedication to shaping a future where progress is not a trade-off but a harmonious integration of human development with the preservation of our planet.

## Cutting-Edge Telecommunications: Weaving the Fabric of Connectivity

In the tapestry of Sudan's transformative journey, telecommunications emerges as the vibrant thread that binds the nation's aspirations. The vision extends far beyond conventional notions of connectivity; it envisions a Sudan where cutting-edge telecommunications redefine how citizens communicate, innovate, and thrive in a globally interconnected world.

Imagine a Sudan where the digital divide is a thing of the past, where high-speed internet is not a luxury but a fundamental right. In this vision, telecommunications become the lifeline that nurtures innovation, empowers individuals, and bridges geographical distances. Sudanese citizens, regardless of their location, find themselves seamlessly connected to the global information highway.

The commitment to cutting-edge telecommunications isn't just about enhancing connectivity; it's about fostering a culture of innovation. Sudan envisions a future where technology isn't a distant marvel but an integral part of everyday life. From smart cities that leverage data for efficient urban planning to educational institutions where digital literacy is a cornerstone, this vision encapsulates a Sudan at the forefront of technological advancement.

As we delve into the realm of cutting-edge telecommunications, the narrative unfolds not just as a story of wires and signals but as a testament to Sudan's determination to empower its citizens. This vision echoes the belief that in an interconnected world, the strength of a nation lies in its ability to adapt, innovate, and seamlessly integrate with the global community.

In weaving the fabric of Sudan's connectivity, telecommunications transcend beyond being a utility; they become the medium through which the nation communicates its dreams, aspirations, and progress to the world. This isn't just about embracing technology; it's about shaping a future where Sudan is not just a participant but a leader in the digital age.

## Water and Sanitation: Nurturing Public Health and Sustainability

In the symphony of Sudan's progress, the chapter of water and sanitation unfolds as a crucial movement, orchestrating a harmonious balance between public health and environmental sustainability. Beyond the provision of basic necessities, Sudan envisions a future where water becomes a cornerstone, not just for survival, but for fostering thriving communities.

Imagine a Sudan where every citizen, regardless of their location, has access to clean and safe water. The vision extends beyond traditional approaches, embracing innovative solutions that not only meet the immediate needs but also ensure the long-term well-being of the population.

Sudan's commitment to water and sanitation goes beyond constructing facilities; it embodies a pledge to nurture public health and create a sustainable environment.

In this vision, sanitation is not an afterthought but an integral part of community planning. Modern waste management systems seamlessly integrate with urban design, ensuring cleanliness becomes a collective responsibility. The pledge is to create not just cities but environments where hygiene is inherent, contributing to the overall well-being of the Sudanese people.

Sudan's dedication to water and sanitation is a testament to its understanding that public health is intertwined with environmental stewardship. It's not just about meeting the immediate needs of the population, but about fostering a sustainable relationship between communities and their surroundings.

As Sudan navigates the waters of progress, it not only ensures that every citizen has access to clean water but also contributes to the preservation of the environment. The pledge is not just to quench the thirst of the present but to sustainably nurture the future, where water and sanitation become catalysts for healthier, cleaner, and more resilient communities. This chapter unfolds not as a mere obligation but as a promise—a promise to weave a future where the ebb and flow of water symbolize not just life but a harmonious coexistence between humanity and the environment.

# Educational Hubs: Cultivating Minds, Shaping Futures

In the saga of Sudan's transformation, the chapter dedicated to educational hubs emerges as a pivotal narrative, defining a future where brilliance is not just encouraged but cultivated. Beyond the conventional view of educational institutions, Sudan envisions vibrant hubs that transcend boundaries, becoming the breeding grounds for innovation, critical thinking, and the shaping of a new generation of leaders.

Imagine educational institutions that stand as architectural marvels, reflecting the grandeur of Sudan's commitment to academic excellence. In this vision, classrooms become not just spaces for lectures but arenas for the exchange of ideas, fostering an environment where curiosity is nurtured, and intellectual growth knows no bounds.

The commitment to educational hubs extends beyond traditional disciplines. Sudan envisions institutions that embrace technology, arts, and sciences, creating a diverse spectrum of knowledge. The vision isn't merely about imparting information; it's about instilling a passion for learning that transcends textbooks and classrooms.

Sudan's dedication to educational excellence is not just a promise to the current generation but a profound investment in the future. It's about creating an environment where students are not just recipients of knowledge but active contributors to the advancement of society. The commitment goes beyond constructing buildings; it involves creating ecosystems where the pursuit of knowledge becomes a way of life.

In this vision, educational hubs are not isolated islands; they are integrated into the fabric of communities, contributing to the socio-economic development of the nation. As Sudan cultivates minds and shapes futures, it ensures that the potential of every individual is recognized and nurtured, contributing to the overall progress of the nation.

As Sudan's educational hubs unfold, they become more than just institutions—they become the crucibles where the nation's intellectual wealth is refined and polished. This chapter is not just about constructing schools and universities; it's about creating legacies, where the pursuit of knowledge becomes a driving force for societal advancement. In the tapestry of Sudan's progress, educational hubs stand as pillars, symbolizing the nation's commitment to brilliance, innovation, and the relentless pursuit of a brighter tomorrow.

## Healthcare Revolution: Nurturing Well-being, Ensuring Equity

Within the grand narrative of Sudan's transformation, the chapter dedicated to the healthcare revolution emerges as a testament to a nation's commitment to the well-being of its citizens. Beyond the conventional view of healthcare, Sudan envisions a system that not only addresses immediate health needs but also ensures equitable access to quality services across the nation.

Imagine state-of-the-art medical facilities dotting the Sudanese landscape, each a beacon of hope and healing. In this vision, healthcare is not merely a service but a fundamental right, accessible to every citizen regardless of their geographic location. The commitment extends beyond treating illnesses; it embodies a pledge to foster a culture of preventative care, ensuring that the health of the nation is proactively safeguarded.

The healthcare revolution is not just about constructing hospitals and clinics; it involves a paradigm shift toward holistic well-being. Sudan envisions a future where healthcare is not a luxury but an integral part of community planning, with a focus on preventative measures, health education, and community engagement.

In this vision, healthcare transcends the confines of traditional medicine. Sudan embraces innovative technologies, telemedicine, and holistic approaches that address not only physical ailments but also mental health. The commitment is not just to cure diseases; it is to create an ecosystem where citizens are actively engaged in maintaining their health and well-being.

As Sudan navigates the healthcare revolution, it ensures that the benefits are not concentrated in urban centers but reach every corner of the nation. The pledge is to reduce disparities, foster health equity, and empower communities to take charge of their well-being. In Sudan's vision, healthcare is not just a reactive response to illnesses; it is a proactive investment in the resilience and vitality of the Sudanese people.

It is a promise—a promise to build a healthcare system that goes beyond treating symptoms to fostering a culture of well-being. It is about creating a future where every citizen, regardless of their background, has the opportunity to lead a healthy and fulfilling life. The healthcare revolution in Sudan is not just about curing ailments; it is about nurturing a nation's most valuable asset—its people.

## Empowering Women: Pioneering Equality, Fostering Leadership

In Sudan's narrative, the chapter dedicated to empowering women takes center stage—a pledge to dismantle barriers, challenge norms, and pave the way for a future where women are not just equal contributors but leaders shaping the destiny of the nation. This commitment goes beyond rhetoric; it is a profound acknowledgment that the empowerment of women is essential for the holistic progress of Sudan.

Imagine a Sudan where women stand at the forefront of decision-making, their voices echoing not just in households but resonating across boardrooms and political arenas. In this vision, empowerment is not merely about granting rights; it involves creating an environment where women are encouraged to pursue education, excel in their careers, and actively participate in shaping societal norms.

Sudan's commitment to empowering women extends beyond legal frameworks; it involves cultural shifts and dismantling stereotypes that have long constrained the potential of half the population. The vision is not just about equality on paper; it is about fostering an inclusive society where every woman, irrespective of her background, has the opportunity to thrive and lead.

In this journey of empowerment, Sudan recognizes the interconnectedness of gender equality with broader societal progress. The empowerment of women becomes a catalyst for economic growth, societal harmony, and the overall advancement of the nation. It's not just about uplifting individuals; it's about harnessing the collective potential of Sudanese women to drive progress.

## Environmental Stewardship: Sustaining Sudan's Natural Riches

As Sudan charts its course toward a sustainable future, the chapter on environmental stewardship emerges as a vital narrative—a pledge to preserve the nation's natural riches for current and future generations. This commitment transcends mere conservation; it is about fostering a symbiotic relationship between humanity and the environment.

Imagine Sudan as a custodian of its own biodiversity, where lush landscapes, vibrant ecosystems, and extraordinary wildlife flourish. In this vision, environmental stewardship is not just a responsibility; it is a deep-seated commitment to sustainable practices, conservation efforts, and policies that safeguard Sudan's natural heritage.

Sudan's commitment to environmental stewardship extends beyond national borders. It envisions a role as a global advocate for sustainable practices, sharing knowledge, and collaborating with the international community to address global environmental challenges. The vision is not just about protecting Sudan's environment; it is about contributing to the well-being of the entire planet.

In this narrative, Sudan embraces renewable energy, advocates for sustainable agriculture, and implements policies that balance economic development with ecological preservation. The commitment is not just to mitigate environmental degradation but to actively contribute to the restoration and rejuvenation of the planet.

As Sudan embraces environmental stewardship, it becomes a guardian of its own destiny. This chapter is not just about safeguarding natural resources; it is about recognizing that the health of the environment is intricately linked to the prosperity and well-being of the Sudanese people. It's a pledge to cultivate a future where Sudan's natural riches continue to thrive, providing sustenance, beauty, and inspiration for generations to come.

## A United Sudan: Embracing the Tapestry of Progress

As we draw the curtains on this chapter of Sudan's visionary transformation, we find ourselves at the intersection of dreams and reality. The tapestry of progress woven through roads, energy revolutions, educational hubs, healthcare reforms, and the empowerment of women comes together in a symphony of collective determination.

Sudan's journey is not a solitary one; it is a narrative crafted by the hands of millions who dare to dream of a brighter tomorrow. Each infrastructure project, every classroom built, and every woman empowered is a stitch in the fabric of a united Sudan—bound not just by geography but by the shared aspirations of its people.

In envisioning a united Sudan, we transcend beyond the tangible achievements. We embrace a unity of purpose, a shared commitment to prosperity, and an unwavering belief that the potential within the Sudanese spirit is boundless. It's not just about constructing buildings; it's about erecting pillars of resilience, determination, and collective progress.

As this chapter concludes, the vision for Sudan stands as a testament to the resilience of a nation that refuses to be defined by its past but instead shapes its destiny with every forward step. The challenges faced are not roadblocks but stepping stones, propelling Sudan into an era where its potential is not just realized but celebrated.

In the tapestry of progress, every endeavor becomes a brushstroke, contributing to a vibrant and dynamic portrait of Sudan's future. The roads become more than thoroughfares; they become the veins of a pulsating nation. The energy revolution becomes more than a transition; it becomes the lifeblood that sustains Sudan's growth. Educational hubs cease to be just buildings; they become the crucibles where brilliance is refined.

As we close this chapter, let us carry forward the spirit of unity, determination, and hope. For in the tapestry of progress, Sudan is not just a nation but a canvas painted with the dreams of its people. The conclusion is not an end but a transition—a transition into a future where the chapters to come will continue to echo the ideals, dreams, and aspirations of a united Sudan.

# Chapter 12: Military

*"Out of every one hundred men, ten shouldn't even be there, eighty are just targets, nine are the real fighters, and we are lucky to have them, for they make the battle. Ah, but the one, one is a warrior, and he will bring the others back."*

– Heraclitus

In the rhythmic heartbeat of a nation, where the echoes of struggles and triumphs resonate through the corridors of history, the warriors emerge from the shadows to carve the destiny of a unified Sudan. Heraclitus' ancient wisdom, echoing through the ages, sets the stage for our exploration into the heart and soul of a military destined not just to defend, but to transform.

As the sun rises over the expanse of Sudan, casting its golden glow upon a land rich with promise, we embark on a journey into the beating heart of the military—a force not just of uniformed soldiers but of resilience, determination, and the unyielding spirit that forges a nation's destiny. This isn't just a tale of warfare; it is a narrative of warriors who weave dreams, architects of a future where freedom reigns supreme.

Join us as we unravel the layers of Sudan's military tapestry, where every thread represents a sacrifice, every color signifies unity, and every stitch binds the nation's aspirations. This is not merely a story of war, but a testament to the warriors who pledge their lives to safeguard a dream—one that envisions a Sudan where the ideals of freedom, diversity, and prosperity flourish against the backdrop of challenges faced and overcome.

Buckle up, dear reader, for we are about to look through the trenches of history, the peaks of sacrifice, and the valleys of resilience. Welcome to the saga of Sudan's warriors—where the battles are not just fought on the front lines but in the hearts and minds of those who dare to dream of a better tomorrow.

## Transformative Military: Guardians of Freedom and Independence

In the vast expanse of Sudan's rich history, the military transcends its conventional role as a guardian of borders; it emerges as the steadfast custodian of dreams, aspirations, and the very essence of a united nation. As we venture deeper into the core of this narrative, we embark on a profound journey through time, bearing witness to the transformative and multifaceted role played by the military in shaping the destiny of a resilient Sudan.

Beyond the uniformed soldiers, the military resembles a mosaic, intricately composed of various elements that converge to create a harmonious and powerful whole. It extends its reach to the veterans who, having weathered the storms of conflict, embody the indomitable spirit that paves the way for a brighter future. These veterans, with their wealth of experience and unwavering commitment, stand as living monuments to the sacrifices made in the pursuit of freedom and unity, linking the past to the present and future.

Civil-military relations form the backbone of a stable and democratic society. In Sudan's narrative, the military stands not only as a formidable defense force but as an independent entity, shielded from undue political influence. This separation ensures that the military's primary focus remains on safeguarding the nation and its citizens. The delicate balance between governance and defense creates an environment where both entities work in tandem, contributing synergistically to the nation's prosperity.

Religious tolerance within the military serves as a microcosm of Sudan's broader ethos. Soldiers from diverse faiths stand shoulder to shoulder, exemplifying a harmonious coexistence that transcends religious differences. The military becomes a living example of the nation it protects, celebrating the freedom of worship and embodying the principles of inclusion and acceptance. This unity within diversity strengthens the fabric of both the military and the nation it serves.

A unique facet emerges as senior citizens find a place of honor within the military structure. Their accumulated wisdom becomes an invaluable asset, contributing not only to national defense but also to the overall development of the nation. Tailored programs designed to harness the experience and knowledge of seniors showcase Sudan's commitment to inclusivity and respect for the older generation, acknowledging their ongoing role in shaping the nation's future.

Amidst the diverse threads that compose Sudan's military tapestry, the nation unequivocally declares zero tolerance for corruption. Integrity and transparency become guiding principles, ensuring that every resource allocated to the military serves its intended purpose—defending the nation and fostering prosperity. Success stories of military leaders actively combating corruption become beacons of hope, signaling a commitment to responsible governance that echoes throughout the nation.

Sudan's military emerges not just as a defender of borders but as a transformative force—unyielding in its dedication to safeguarding the principles of freedom, independence, and unity. The tapestry of Sudan's military is intricately woven with threads of sacrifice, resilience, and a collective commitment to a brighter tomorrow. As the saga continues, the warriors stand ready, for theirs is a journey that transcends time, shaping the destiny of a nation on the rise.

# Veterans' Contribution: Upholding the Spirit of Sacrifice

In the ongoing narrative of Sudan's military evolution, this segment pays homage to the invaluable contributions of veterans, embodying the spirit of sacrifice that has indelibly shaped the nation's history. These individuals stand as living monuments, having weathered the trials of war and conflict in the service of their nation. Sudan envisions a future where the sacrifices of these esteemed individuals are not only recognized but actively harnessed for the nation's ongoing development.

The military recognizes that veterans bring a wealth of experience, skills, and resilience forged in the crucible of conflict. Their commitment to Sudan's ideals extends beyond their time in active service, and as such, initiatives are introduced to provide comprehensive support for veterans' well-being. This includes robust healthcare services that address both physical and mental health needs, acknowledging that the effects of war can linger long after the battlefield.

Moreover, Sudan's military becomes a facilitator for veterans' smooth reintegration into civilian life. Transitioning from a military to civilian context can pose unique challenges, and thus, tailored programs are implemented to ensure that veterans not only reintegrate successfully but also thrive in their post-service lives.

Educational and vocational training opportunities are offered, tapping into the potential of veterans to contribute meaningfully to the nation's progress.

Recognizing that veterans serve as a bridge between the past and the future, the military values their role in mentorship programs. Through these initiatives, the experiences of veterans become a source of inspiration for the younger generation, fostering a sense of unity, resilience, and a shared commitment to Sudan's enduring values.

Beyond individual support, the military encourages collective endeavors that showcase the ongoing contributions of veterans. Their involvement in community projects, national events, and cultural initiatives serves to highlight the enduring impact of their service. Sudan's military aims not only to acknowledge the sacrifices of its veterans but actively invests in their continued well-being, ensuring that their legacy remains a guiding force in the nation's journey towards prosperity and unity.

## Building Bridges: Unity through International Collaboration

In the evolution of Sudan's military narrative, this chapter unfolds as a dedicated exploration of building bridges—forging connections and fostering unity through strategic international collaboration. As we delve into this section, we discover how alliances, partnerships, and shared endeavors become the keystones in the foundation of a globally connected and empowered Sudan.

Sudan envisions a future where diplomatic alliances transcend geographical boundaries, creating a network of support and collaboration. The military becomes a catalyst for international dialogue, fostering relationships built on mutual respect and shared interests. These alliances extend beyond traditional military cooperation, encompassing diplomatic, economic, and cultural ties that contribute to the nation's global standing.

Through joint military exercises, training programs, and intelligence sharing, Sudan's military not only enhances its own capabilities but also strengthens the bonds with allied nations. Such collaborations act as a force multiplier, ensuring that Sudan is not isolated but stands shoulder to shoulder with its international counterparts.

Economic partnerships form a crucial aspect of this global vision. Sudan recognizes that economic strength is intertwined with national security. By engaging in joint economic ventures, trade agreements, and infrastructure projects with partner nations, the military becomes a driving force in propelling Sudan's economic growth. These partnerships not only benefit the nation's prosperity but also create a more stable and interconnected global landscape.

Cultural exchanges play a pivotal role in fostering understanding and unity. The military actively engages in programs that promote cultural diplomacy, showcasing Sudan's rich heritage to the world and embracing the diversity offered by its international partners. These cultural bonds go beyond borders, creating a shared sense of identity and pride.

International collaboration is not merely a strategic choice but a reflection of Sudan's commitment to addressing global challenges. Sudan's military actively participates in peacekeeping missions, humanitarian endeavors, and efforts to combat transnational threats. By contributing to global security and stability, Sudan solidifies its role as a responsible member of the international community.

The vision is clear—a Sudan that is not isolated but intricately woven into the fabric of global affairs. The military emerges as a bridge-builder, connecting Sudan with the world through diplomacy, economics, and shared cultural experiences. In this interconnected future, Sudan stands united with the international community, contributing to a world where collaboration triumphs over isolation.

## Religious Tolerance within the Military: Unity Beyond Beliefs

In the intricate tapestry of Sudan's military vision, this segment delves into the profound importance of religious tolerance within the armed forces. The chapter unfolds as a testament to Sudan's commitment to fostering unity beyond religious beliefs, recognizing that diversity can be a source of strength rather than division.

The military envisions a future where individuals from diverse religious backgrounds coexist harmoniously, bound by a shared commitment to the nation's security and prosperity. Sudan recognizes that religious diversity within the military enriches its fabric, bringing varied perspectives, values, and traditions that collectively contribute to a more robust and resilient armed forces.

Initiatives are introduced to ensure that religious tolerance is not only embraced but actively promoted within the military culture. Training programs focus on fostering an understanding of different religious practices, beliefs, and cultural nuances. The goal is to create an environment where each member of the military feels respected and valued, irrespective of their faith.

Religious accommodation becomes a cornerstone of this vision, ensuring that individuals can practice their faith without fear of discrimination. Prayer spaces, observance of religious holidays, and dietary considerations are integrated into the military framework, fostering an inclusive environment where everyone can fully participate in both their religious and military duties.

The military actively discourages any form of discrimination based on religious beliefs, fostering a culture where individuals are judged on their merits and contributions rather than their faith. By doing so, Sudan's armed forces become a shining example of how diversity can be harnessed as a source of strength and unity.

Sudan's military not only recognizes the importance of religious tolerance but actively strives to create an inclusive environment where individuals from all faiths can stand united in their dedication to the nation. By embracing diversity, Sudan ensures that its armed forces are not just defenders of borders but champions of unity and understanding.

## Honoring Legacy: Senior Citizens' Integral Role in Sudan's Military

In the evolving chapters of Sudan's military narrative, VI delves into a poignant exploration of the integral role played by senior citizens within the armed forces. This segment unfolds as a tribute to the wealth of experience, wisdom, and unwavering dedication that older generations bring to the military landscape.

Sudan envisions a military that not only respects but actively integrates senior citizens into its fabric. These individuals, having weathered the storms of history, embody a living legacy of the nation's struggles and triumphs. The military seeks to leverage this invaluable repository of experience, recognizing that the past is not a burden but a guiding light toward a more resilient and informed future.

Initiatives are set in motion to create roles within the military structure that harness the unique skills and insights of senior citizens. While combat roles may transition to the younger generation, seniors find meaningful positions in mentorship, strategic planning, and administrative capacities. This deliberate integration serves a dual purpose: it honors the legacy of those who have served and ensures that their wealth of knowledge actively contributes to the military's ongoing mission.

Moreover, programs aimed at the well-being of senior citizens within the military are established. These encompass healthcare provisions, recreational activities, and community engagement, recognizing that a cared-for and respected senior population is an asset to the entire military community.

Beyond the practical contributions, the inclusion of senior citizens in the military serves as a powerful symbol of continuity and unity. It reinforces the idea that the military is not just an institution but a living organism, adapting and evolving while remaining grounded in the principles that have shaped Sudan's history.

Sudan's military emerges not only as a defender of borders but as a custodian of its own history. By honoring the legacy of senior citizens, Sudan paves the way for a military that bridges generational gaps, ensuring that the lessons of the past are not forgotten as the nation forges ahead into a promising future.

## Zero Tolerance for Corruption: Safeguarding Sudan's Integrity

In the unfolding narrative of Sudan's military vision, this chapter stands as a stalwart declaration against corruption, emphasizing a commitment to maintaining the highest standards of integrity within the armed forces. It represents Sudan's unwavering stance that a nation's progress is intricately tied to the eradication of corruption from its institutions.

The military envisions a future where every facet of its operations, from financial management to personnel conduct, is characterized by transparency, accountability, and an unequivocal rejection of corrupt practices. Sudan recognizes that corruption not only undermines the effectiveness of the armed forces but erodes public trust and hampers the nation's overall development.

Initiatives are launched to instill a culture of ethical conduct and integrity within the military ranks. Anti-corruption training becomes an integral part of military education, emphasizing the importance of upholding the nation's values and the duty to serve with honor. Soldiers are not just defenders of borders; they are stewards of Sudan's integrity.

The military implements stringent measures and internal controls to detect and prevent corruption. Comprehensive audits, transparent financial practices, and whistleblower protection programs are put in place to ensure that any malfeasance is swiftly identified and addressed. By doing so, Sudan's armed forces become a bastion of accountability, demonstrating a commitment to safeguarding the nation's resources and reputation.

A robust legal framework is established to prosecute and penalize corrupt practices within the military. Sudan recognizes that accountability is a cornerstone of a corruption-free institution, and the military actively collaborates with legal authorities to ensure that those who engage in corrupt activities are held responsible for their actions.

Sudan's military not only declares its zero-tolerance stance towards corruption but actively implements measures to foster a culture of integrity. By doing so, the armed forces become a beacon of trust, ensuring that every citizen can take pride in an institution that not only defends the nation but upholds the principles of transparency, accountability, and ethical conduct.

## Unity Against Terrorism: Fortifying Sudan's Defenses

In the intricate tapestry of Sudan's military vision, this chapter underscores the imperative of unity against terrorism—a resolute commitment to fortify the nation's defenses and protect its citizens from the scourge of terrorism. It serves as a testament to Sudan's unwavering stance that a united front is the most potent weapon against the forces that seek to destabilize and threaten peace.

The military envisions a future where unity prevails over division, where diverse communities stand shoulder to shoulder, resolute in their determination to eradicate terrorism from Sudan's soil. Recognizing that terrorism knows no boundaries, Sudan aims to forge a comprehensive strategy that unites citizens, military forces, and international partners against this common threat.

Initiatives are introduced to enhance intelligence capabilities, fostering a collaborative approach between military and civilian entities. The goal is to create a network of vigilance that can swiftly identify and neutralize any terrorist threat. Sudan's military actively engages in intelligence-sharing agreements, recognizing that a united global effort is essential to combating the transnational nature of terrorism.

Counterterrorism training becomes a cornerstone of military preparedness. Soldiers are equipped not only with the physical skills needed to address terrorist threats but also with a deep understanding of the ideologies that fuel such acts. The military aims to be a force that not only reacts to terrorism but actively works to prevent radicalization and extremism within its ranks and communities.

The military collaborates closely with law enforcement agencies, creating a seamless integration of efforts to combat terrorism. Joint operations, information sharing, and coordinated responses become standard practices, ensuring that Sudan's defenses are robust and adaptive to the evolving tactics employed by terrorist organizations.

Sudan recognizes the importance of international collaboration in the fight against terrorism. The military actively participates in regional and global initiatives, fostering alliances that strengthen the collective resolve against this common enemy. By doing so, Sudan aims not only to secure its own borders but to contribute to a safer world where terrorism finds no sanctuary.

Sudan's military not only declares its commitment to unity against terrorism but actively implements measures to fortify the nation's defenses. By fostering collaboration at national and international levels, Sudan stands as a beacon of resilience, sending a clear message that the forces of unity will always triumph over the forces of terror.

## Conclusion: A Unified Sudan, Forging a Resilient Future

As we draw the final strokes in the canvas of Sudan's military vision, the conclusion emerges as a resounding affirmation of a unified nation forging a resilient future. This chapter encapsulates the essence of Sudan's journey, highlighting the transformative aspirations that propel the armed forces and its citizens toward a prosperous and harmonious tomorrow.

The military's vision for Sudan is not merely a collection of ideals; it is a roadmap for the nation's evolution. It envisions a future where the echoes of the past, the sacrifices of veterans, and the resilience of the people converge to create a tapestry of unity and progress. Sudan stands as a beacon of hope, demonstrating that even in the face of historical challenges, a united nation can carve out a destiny that transcends expectations.

The core principles of this vision—religious tolerance, zero tolerance for corruption, unity against terrorism, and the inclusion of veterans and senior citizens—represent Sudan's commitment to building an inclusive and equitable society. The military serves not just as a defender of borders but as a catalyst for positive change, actively engaging in initiatives that elevate the nation's values and aspirations.

As Sudan strides into the future, the conclusion reiterates the importance of collective effort. It acknowledges that the journey towards prosperity requires the dedication and collaboration of every citizen, whether within the military ranks or in civilian life. Sudan's armed forces envision a nation where the ideals of unity, integrity, and resilience are not just spoken of but lived and breathed by every Sudanese.

In closing, the conclusion extends an invitation to every citizen to contribute to the realization of this vision. It is a call to action, urging individuals to stand united, to embrace diversity, and to uphold the principles that define Sudan's unique identity. The military's vision is not a static document; it is a living testament to Sudan's unwavering spirit—a spirit that propels the nation forward into a future marked by unity, progress, and enduring resilience.

# Chapter 13: Law & Order

In the vibrant mosaic of Sudan's history, the pulsating rhythm of law and order resonates like a melody that refuses to be forgotten. It's a dance – a graceful intertwining of tradition and progress, where the echoes of ancient legal systems twirl with the contemporary beats of a nation in metamorphosis. Envision stepping into a realm where time bends, and the past, present, and future converge on the stage of justice.

Imagine the ancient alleys of Sudan, where elders gathered under the shade of acacia trees, settling disputes through the wisdom of customary laws. Here, justice wore the cloak of tradition, and the elders, like guardians of ancestral knowledge, ensured the harmony of their communities. Yet, time marches forward, and so does the need for adaptation.

The stage transitions to a bustling modern city, where courtrooms hum with the cadence of legal debates and the tap-tap of keyboards. Picture a young lawyer, armed not only with statutes but also with the echoes of his ancestors' stories. In this scenario, tradition and modernity dance in unison, a testament to Sudan's complex legal journey.

This chapter is an invitation to witness the fusion of two worlds, where we explore the intricacies of traditional legal systems and trace the footsteps of Sudan's legal evolution. The dance floor is vast, and each step forward reveals a narrative that transcends time. The tapestry unfolds, depicting challenges faced and victories celebrated, weaving a narrative of a nation on the brink of a legal revolution.

Picture a scenario where a community grapples with a conflict. The elders, deeply rooted in tradition, convene beneath the acacia trees to find resolution. Meanwhile, a legal scholar armed with contemporary legal knowledge collaborates with them, seeking a harmony that honors both past and present. It's a moment frozen in time, symbolizing the delicate balance Sudan strives to achieve.

This chapter is more than words on a page; it's an immersive experience into Sudan's legal odyssey. It beckons you to join the dance, where the past and the future swirl together, creating a vision of justice that transcends the ordinary. As the curtain rises, the spotlight is on Sudan – a nation poised for a legal revolution, where the dance of law and order choreographs a symphony of transformation.

## The Evolution of Legal Systems

As we traverse the historical landscape of Sudan, the evolution of legal systems emerges as a captivating narrative, akin to a river flowing through changing terrains. Imagine standing on the banks of this river, where the waters of tradition and modernity converge, creating a dynamic ecosystem of justice.

In the early chapters of Sudan's legal saga, the ancient traditions painted the canvas of justice with hues drawn from the earth itself. Beneath the towering acacia trees, elders convened to unravel disputes, employing customary laws that were not just rules but living embodiments of community ethos. It was a decentralized legal symphony, where justice was dispensed with an intimacy born of shared history.

As time's relentless current flowed, Sudan found itself at the crossroads of tradition and progress. The colonial era introduced foreign legal structures, bringing a paradigm shift that challenged the very foundations of indigenous systems. Picture the clash of two tides – the familiar cadence of tribal councils facing the authoritative gavel of a foreign court. Sudan's legal identity became a patchwork quilt, stitched with threads of both continuity and change.

Fast forward to the present, and the legal landscape is a mosaic reflecting Sudan's resilience. It's a narrative of adaptation, where the country, like a skilled navigator, steers through the currents of globalization without losing sight of its roots. In courtrooms adorned with symbols of a nation's struggle, contemporary legal professionals navigate the complexities of a legal system that is both a legacy and a response to the demands of the modern era.

In this evolving legal tapestry, imagine conversations between generations. Elders pass down the stories of under the acacia trees, infused with the wisdom of tradition, to young legal minds who, in turn, blend it with the vigor of contemporary knowledge. It's a dialogue that bridges the temporal gap, a conversation that embraces the continuum of Sudan's legal evolution.

As we reflect on the evolution of legal systems in Sudan, envision a nation on the brink of a legal renaissance. The river of justice, with its twists and turns, symbolizes not just the journey but the destination – a Sudan that respects its heritage while navigating the currents of a dynamic future. The evolution continues, a testament to the resilience of a nation that dances on the precipice of legal transformation.

## Justice and Equality

In the heart of Sudan's legal metamorphosis lies a profound exploration of justice and equality, an odyssey that transcends mere courtroom proceedings to touch the very soul of a nation. Picture a courthouse where the scales of justice not only weigh evidence but also bear the weight of a society's aspirations for fairness and impartiality.

Justice, in the Sudanese context, is not merely a legal concept; it's a cultural ethos, woven into the fabric of community life. As we journey through the historical alleys, imagine elders beneath the acacia trees, dispensing justice with a keen understanding of the communal pulse. This early form of justice, rooted in tradition, emphasized restoration and reconciliation over punitive measures.

Fast forward to the present, and the concept of justice undergoes a dynamic shift, navigating the complex currents of a modern legal system. Picture a courtroom adorned with symbols of Sudan's struggle for independence, where judges and legal practitioners grapple with the challenge of aligning legal proceedings with the principles of fairness. The call for justice echoes not just in legal chambers but resonates through the streets, where citizens yearn for a system that is equitable and unbiased.

Equality, like a guiding star, illuminates the path to justice. In Sudan's legal evolution, it becomes a beacon that lights the way forward. Envision a legal framework that acknowledges and addresses historical injustices, striving to rectify imbalances that may have been perpetuated through time. This is not just about legal reform; it's a societal commitment to ensuring that every individual, regardless of background, stands on equal footing before the law.

In the intricate dance of justice and equality, imagine a scenario where a marginalized community seeks recourse. The courtroom becomes a theater where legal professionals, driven by a commitment to fairness, work tirelessly to rectify historical wrongs. It's a moment where the pursuit of justice becomes a collective endeavor, transcending the confines of the legal system to become a societal aspiration.

It is a canvas where justice and equality are not static ideals but evolving principles. The acacia trees may have witnessed a different form of justice, but today's Sudan aspires to redefine these principles for a contemporary era.

The scales of justice tip not just towards legality but towards a society where justice and equality intertwine, creating a harmonious melody that resonates through the corridors of Sudan's legal landscape.

## Legal Education and Empowerment

In the evolving narrative of Sudan's legal landscape, the spotlight now turns to the transformative realm of legal education and empowerment. It's a chapter where the ink on legal documents meets the fervor of knowledge dissemination, envisioning a society where legal literacy becomes not just a privilege but a powerful tool for empowerment.

Picture the transition from acacia-shaded gatherings to the hallowed halls of legal academia. Sudan's journey in legal education mirrors its commitment to forging a new path. In the earlier days, knowledge was passed down through oral traditions, and the elders, as repositories of legal wisdom, held the key to communal harmony. Today, imagine the vibrancy of law schools, where eager minds soak in the complexities of legal frameworks, driven by a passion to contribute to the evolving legal narrative.

Legal education, in this context, is not confined to textbooks and classrooms. It's a dynamic process that engages communities, instilling legal literacy as a fundamental right. Envision a scenario where legal scholars, inspired by a commitment to justice, venture beyond the ivory towers to bridge the gap between academic knowledge and grassroots understanding. The acacia trees, once the stage for legal discourse, now share their shade with legal educators reaching out to communities, emphasizing that the power of law belongs to all.

Empowerment through legal education extends beyond the boundaries of academic institutions. It's about nurturing a generation of legal minds who not only understand the intricacies of statutes but are also passionate about using this knowledge to foster societal well-being. Picture a young lawyer, armed not just with legal codes but with a deep understanding of community needs, playing a pivotal role in resolving disputes and contributing to the social fabric.

In Sudan's legal odyssey, legal education becomes a vehicle for societal transformation. It's a commitment to inclusivity, where legal knowledge is not hoarded but shared generously. Imagine a scenario where legal education becomes a catalyst for community development, empowering individuals to navigate the legal landscape with confidence and contributing to the collective pursuit of justice.

As we navigate, it's not just about legal education; it's about empowerment. The acacia trees, witnesses to Sudan's legal evolution, stand tall, their branches reaching out to embrace a society where legal literacy is not a privilege for the few but a right for all. This is a vision where the power of law is wielded not only by legal professionals in courtrooms but by every citizen empowered through the gift of legal education.

## Community Policing and Engagement

In the unfolding narrative of Sudan's legal progression, the spotlight now illuminates the transformative domain of community policing and engagement. Picture a landscape where law enforcement transcends the traditional role of authority, becoming a collaborative effort that intertwines with the pulse of communities.

In the early chapters of Sudan's legal tale, community policing was an inherent part of the social fabric. Elders, under the shade of acacia trees, played a dual role as keepers of justice and custodians of community safety. Imagine a scenario where the guardianship of law was not a distant concept but a shared responsibility, with everyone contributing to the well-being of the collective.

Fast forward to the present, and community policing takes on a new dimension. Picture a bustling neighborhood where police officers are not just enforcers of the law but allies in community welfare. Sudan's contemporary law enforcement, inspired by the principles of community policing, envisions officers as approachable figures, working hand in hand with citizens to create safe and thriving neighborhoods.

Envision a scenario where law enforcement professionals actively engage with communities, not just during times of crisis but as a continuous effort to build trust. The acacia trees, once the backdrop of legal gatherings, now witness a different dialogue – one where community members and police officers collaborate to identify and address concerns, fostering an environment where justice is not a distant ideal but a shared endeavor.

Community engagement in law enforcement is not merely a concept; it's a living reality where neighborhoods actively participate in shaping their safety. Picture citizens, armed with legal awareness, actively contributing to crime prevention initiatives. It's a scenario where the lines between law enforcement and community blur, creating a dynamic partnership that goes beyond reactive measures to proactive, community-driven solutions.

As we immerse ourselves in this chapter, community policing becomes more than a strategy; it's a philosophy. It's about recognizing that the guardianship of justice is a collective responsibility, and the acacia trees, standing witness to Sudan's evolution, echo with the spirit of cooperation. This is a vision where law enforcement is not an external force but an integral part of the community, where the pursuit of justice is not solitary but a shared dance between those who enforce the law and those it protects.

# Technological Advancements in Law Enforcement

In the symphony of Sudan's legal progression, the stage now transforms to spotlight the dynamic realm of technological advancements in law enforcement. Imagine a landscape where digital innovation becomes not just a tool but a cornerstone in the architecture of justice, reshaping the way society navigates the complexities of maintaining order.

As Sudan's legal narrative unfolds, the scenario transitions from traditional legal practices beneath the acacia trees to a futuristic vision where technology stands as a stalwart ally in the pursuit of justice. Picture a digital landscape where law enforcement professionals leverage cutting-edge tools to ensure the safety and security of communities.

Envision a scenario where surveillance cameras, once an unfamiliar concept, now dot urban landscapes, acting as vigilant guardians of public spaces. Sudan's law enforcement, inspired by technological advancements, uses artificial intelligence to analyze patterns, swiftly identifying potential threats and preventing crime before it occurs. The acacia trees, now accompanied by surveillance towers, silently bear witness to this seamless integration of tradition and technology.

Imagine a world where law enforcement databases are interconnected, enabling swift and efficient information sharing between agencies. This interconnectedness transcends geographical boundaries, creating a network that not only aids in solving crimes but also ensures a collaborative approach to addressing challenges that may span regions.

In this futuristic landscape, picture a scenario where officers equipped with body cameras not only document their interactions but contribute to building a transparent and accountable legal system. It's a vision where technology becomes a bridge between law enforcement and the community, fostering a relationship built on trust and transparency.

Technological advancements become more than tools; they become enablers of a society that aspires to create a safer and more just environment. The acacia trees, symbols of Sudan's past, now cast shadows on a digital frontier where the pursuit of justice is propelled by the innovations of the future. This is a vision where the marriage of tradition and technology forms the backbone of a legal system that not only adapts to the demands of the contemporary world but also paves the way for a safer and more secure Sudan.

## Rehabilitation and Restorative Justice

As the legal narrative of Sudan continues to unfold, the spotlight now turns to the transformative sphere of rehabilitation and restorative justice. Picture a landscape where the traditional punitive approach to law takes a backseat, making room for a more compassionate and holistic vision that seeks to mend the social fabric torn by criminal acts.

In earlier times, justice was often synonymous with punishment, a retribution-centric approach that sought to mete out penalties rather than address the root causes of criminal behavior. Now, envision a shift in perspective where the acacia trees, once silent observers of trials and punishments, witness a paradigm that prioritizes healing and societal reintegration.

In this scenario, imagine a rehabilitation center where individuals convicted of crimes are not merely incarcerated but provided with opportunities for personal growth and redemption. Sudan's commitment to restorative justice envisions a system that recognizes the humanity even in those who have transgressed societal norms, aiming not just for punishment but for the restoration of individuals to productive members of the community.

As we delve into this chapter, envision a dialogue between offenders and the communities they affected. Restorative justice emphasizes the importance of repairing the harm caused, not just through punitive measures, but through active participation and acknowledgment of responsibility. Picture a scenario where communities actively engage in the rehabilitation process, fostering an environment that encourages understanding and forgiveness.

Imagine a world where the legal system prioritizes the reintegration of offenders into society, providing them with skills and support systems that reduce the likelihood of recidivism. Sudan's commitment to rehabilitation becomes a beacon of hope, offering a second chance to those who have erred, with the acacia trees standing witness to a vision where justice is not only blind but compassionate.

Rehabilitation and restorative justice become the pillars of a legal system that seeks not just to punish but to heal. The acacia trees, symbols of wisdom and endurance, watch over a legal evolution that recognizes the potential for redemption in every individual, fostering a society that believes in the power of rehabilitation to mend the fractures caused by crime.

## International Collaboration

In the ongoing narrative of Sudan's legal evolution, the spotlight now turns to the collaborative horizon of international engagement. Picture a canvas where the borders of justice extend beyond national boundaries, fostering a collective approach to addressing global challenges and enriching Sudan's legal fabric.

Sudan, standing at the crossroads of tradition and modernity, recognizes that the pursuit of justice extends beyond its borders. Envision a scenario where legal professionals engage in cross-cultural dialogues, sharing insights, and learning from diverse legal systems. The acacia trees, once silent witnesses to local legal proceedings, now stand in the midst of a global legal symposium.

In this interconnected world, Sudan actively collaborates with international partners, participating in forums that promote the exchange of legal knowledge and expertise. Picture a scenario where Sudanese legal scholars contribute to global discussions on human rights, offering a perspective shaped by the nation's rich cultural heritage and evolving legal practices.

As Sudan embraces international collaboration, envision a partnership that goes beyond theoretical discussions. Imagine legal practitioners from different corners of the globe actively participating in training programs, sharing best practices, and collectively addressing challenges that span international borders. The acacia trees, rooted in Sudanese soil, now share their shade with legal professionals from around the world.

It is a testament to Sudan's commitment to a legal system that is not insular but embraces the benefits of global collaboration. Envision a scenario where Sudan actively contributes to international legal frameworks, ensuring that its unique experiences and challenges are part of the global conversation on justice, human rights, and the rule of law.

As the acacia trees cast their shadows over this collaborative landscape, Sudan's legal system becomes a mosaic woven with threads of international wisdom. The nation stands not as an isolated entity but as an active participant in a global legal community, where the pursuit of justice is a shared endeavor that transcends borders, cultures, and legal traditions.

As we draw the curtains on this chapter of Sudan's legal odyssey, the tapestry woven is one of resilience, transformation, and a commitment to justice. From the shade of acacia trees, where elders once dispensed communal wisdom, to the global legal symposiums where Sudan actively engages with the international legal community, the journey has been one of profound evolution.

The evolution of Sudan's legal systems, the pursuit of justice and equality, the transformative power of legal education and empowerment, the embrace of community policing and engagement, the integration of technological advancements, the shift towards rehabilitation and restorative justice—all underscore a nation's dedication to crafting a legal narrative that resonates with both tradition and innovation.

International collaboration, as witnessed in the closing scenes, paints Sudan as an active participant in a global legal discourse. The acacia trees, standing tall, symbolize not just the roots of Sudanese legal heritage but also the far-reaching branches that connect with legal communities worldwide. The pursuit of justice becomes a shared journey, where borders dissolve, and collective wisdom shapes the future.

In summary, Sudan emerges not merely as a nation with a legal system but as a participant in the global legal narrative, contributing its unique hues to the palette of justice. As the story unfolds, the vision becomes clear—a Sudan where justice is not a destination but an ongoing journey, where the legal landscape, like the acacia trees, stands resilient against the winds of change.

In the chapters to come, the journey continues, and the legal narrative of Sudan remains an open book, waiting to be written with the ink of innovation, compassion, and a collective commitment to shaping a future where justice, in all its forms, becomes the cornerstone of a thriving nation.

# Chapter 14: Communism vs. Capitalism in the Sudanese Context

In the tapestry of Sudanese aspirations, the threads of political ideologies weave a narrative crucial to the nation's transformative journey. As we embark on a contemplative exploration of Communism and Capitalism, let us be guided by the words of wisdom echoing through time: *"In the pursuit of a united Sudan, the canvas of political ideologies becomes a masterpiece, blending hues of collectivism and individualism."*

Communism and Capitalism, each a distinctive brushstroke on the canvas of governance, carry histories rich with global implications. In understanding their dynamic interplay, we unfold a chapter in Sudanese history that holds the promise of unity and prosperity. This exploration becomes essential in sculpting a Sudanese identity that transcends historical divides and shapes a future where the dreams and visions of the people come to fruition.

To comprehend the significance of these ideologies, we must first appreciate their historical roots and global impact. Communism, born from the crucible of social inequality, seeks collective ownership and societal equality. Capitalism, a product of the human spirit's entrepreneurial drive, thrives on economic freedom and individual prosperity. These ideologies, seemingly at odds, find themselves entwined in the complex tapestry of Sudan's socio-political landscape.

As we delve into the historical evolution of Communism and Capitalism, we lay the foundation for a nuanced understanding of their application within the unique context of Sudan. The historical context acts as a compass, guiding us through the labyrinth of ideologies and setting the stage for a discussion that transcends theoretical debates to address the practical needs of Sudanese society.

This exploration is not a mere academic exercise; rather, it is a journey towards pragmatic solutions for a nation seeking not only political stability but also social cohesion. The interconnectedness of these ideologies becomes apparent as we dissect their principles and envision a Sudanese model that harmonizes the collective spirit of Communism with the dynamic innovation of Capitalism.

In the chapters that follow, we will navigate the landscapes of Communism and Capitalism, uncovering their potential roles in reshaping Sudan's political and economic future. The overarching goal is not to advocate for one over the other but to discern a path forward that amalgamates the strengths of both ideologies. As we step into the heart of this discourse, let us be guided by the belief that in the fusion of political ideals lies the key to a united and prosperous Sudan.

# Communism: A Collective Vision for a Unified Sudan

Communism, as a socio-political ideology, extends an invitation to envision Sudan as a collective, unified entity. Rooted in the principle of collective ownership, it emerges as a potential catalyst for addressing historical disparities that have plagued the nation. By advocating for the equitable distribution of resources and dismantling socio-economic hierarchies, Communism presents itself as a force capable of fostering social cohesion and unity.

In the Sudanese context, where historical divisions have often hindered progress, Communism offers a collective vision that transcends tribal, ethnic, and regional boundaries. It seeks to bridge the gaps between the privileged and the marginalized, fostering a sense of shared responsibility for the nation's well-being. By emphasizing the importance of communal ownership, Communism aligns with the intrinsic values of unity and solidarity deeply embedded in Sudanese culture.

This ideology carries the potential to address not only economic disparities but also historical injustices. The scars of past conflicts, fueled by economic imbalances and social inequalities, could find healing in the collective embrace of Communist ideals. The concept of shared resources, when applied judiciously, has the capacity to uplift marginalized communities, empowering them to actively contribute to Sudan's progress.

Internationally, we find examples where socialist policies have successfully leveled the playing field and created societies with reduced wealth gaps. Sudan can draw inspiration from these instances, tailoring Communist principles to suit its unique socio-political landscape. The aim is not to transplant an ideology wholesale but to adapt its principles to address the specific needs of a nation yearning for unity.

Moreover, Communism's emphasis on collective decision-making aligns with the Sudanese aspiration for inclusive governance. By involving citizens in the decision-making processes, Sudan can forge a path towards a more participatory democracy, fostering a sense of ownership and accountability among its people. This participatory approach resonates with the call for a united Sudan where every voice contributes to the nation's destiny.

Communism, then, is not just an economic system; it is a philosophy that can infuse a sense of purpose and shared destiny into the Sudanese psyche. It has the potential to redefine the narrative of a fragmented past, offering a collective vision that unites Sudanese citizens under the common banner of shared prosperity and social justice.

As we navigate through the intricacies of Communist ideals, let us envision a Sudan where the collective spirit supersedes divisive tendencies, and the pursuit of a unified nation becomes a reality rather than a distant dream.

## Capitalism: Economic Prosperity and Individual Freedom

In juxtaposition to Communism's emphasis on collective ownership, Capitalism emerges as an ideology rooted in individualism and economic freedom. For Sudan, a nation aspiring to rise from historical challenges, Capitalism presents an enticing prospect of economic prosperity and individual empowerment.

At its core, Capitalism celebrates the entrepreneurial spirit, encouraging individuals to harness their innovative potential to spur economic growth. Sudan, with its vast untapped resources and potential, stands to benefit from a system that places a premium on individual initiative and private enterprise. The dynamism inherent in a free-market economy can serve as a powerful engine for development, stimulating innovation and fostering a climate of economic vibrancy.

The concept of private property ownership, a cornerstone of Capitalism, holds particular relevance for Sudan's economic landscape. By promoting individual ownership and investment, Capitalism encourages a sense of responsibility and accountability. This ethos aligns with the Sudanese aspiration for economic autonomy, allowing citizens to actively contribute to the nation's progress through entrepreneurial ventures and investments.

Furthermore, the experience of successful capitalist economies around the world provides valuable lessons for Sudan. Nations that have embraced market-driven development have often witnessed rapid economic growth and increased standards of living. The potential benefits extend beyond mere financial gains; they include the establishment of a robust economic infrastructure that can sustain long-term development initiatives.

Capitalism's commitment to individual freedom aligns with Sudan's quest for a society where citizens can exercise their agency to shape their destinies. The freedom to pursue economic opportunities, make individual choices, and benefit from the fruits of one's labor resonates with the Sudanese desire for personal empowerment. In a nation striving for unity and progress, empowering individuals economically can contribute to a collective sense of pride and ownership in the nation's success.

While acknowledging the merits of Capitalism, it is crucial to recognize its potential pitfalls, such as income inequality and the exploitation of resources. Therefore, the application of Capitalist principles in Sudan must be approached with a nuanced understanding, ensuring that economic prosperity is inclusive and sustainable, benefiting all strata of society.

In navigating the landscape of Capitalism, Sudan can draw inspiration from global success stories, tailoring its economic policies to suit its unique context. A judicious blend of free-market dynamics and socially responsible governance could pave the way for a Sudanese economic renaissance.

As we explore the tenets of Capitalism, envision Sudan not just as a nation with economic potential but as a society where the entrepreneurial spirit of its individuals fuels a collective journey towards prosperity and self-determination.

## The Need for Balance: Synthesizing Communism and Capitalism

As we traverse the ideological landscape, it becomes apparent that an exclusive allegiance to either Communism or Capitalism may fall short of addressing Sudan's complex socio-political fabric. The call for a balanced synthesis arises from the understanding that each ideology carries its strengths and weaknesses, and it is in the delicate interplay between them that Sudan may find a path forward.

Communism, with its focus on collective ownership and social equality, provides a lens through which historical injustices can be rectified and societal disparities addressed. It holds the potential to create a foundation of shared prosperity, binding the diverse fabric of Sudanese society together. However, an unbridled adherence to Communist principles may risk stifling individual initiative and innovation, hampering economic growth.

On the other hand, Capitalism, with its emphasis on individual freedom and economic dynamism, presents an opportunity for Sudan to tap into the entrepreneurial spirit of its citizens. A market-driven economy can catalyze rapid development, create job opportunities, and elevate living standards. However, the unchecked pursuit of profit under a purely Capitalist system may exacerbate income inequality and sideline marginalized communities.

The synthesis of these ideologies in Sudanese governance requires a nuanced approach. A model that incorporates elements of both Communism and Capitalism can harness the strengths of each while mitigating their respective shortcomings. By doing so, Sudan can build a society that is economically vibrant, socially just, and politically inclusive.

The key lies in identifying where each ideology can contribute most effectively. Communism's principles of collective ownership can be channeled into sectors that are fundamental to societal well-being, such as healthcare, education, and basic infrastructure. By ensuring universal access to these essential services, Sudan can build a solid foundation for collective progress and unity.

Simultaneously, the entrepreneurial spirit encouraged by Capitalism can find expression in sectors where innovation and competition are catalysts for growth. A thriving private sector can stimulate economic development, create employment opportunities, and foster a culture of individual responsibility.

Moreover, the synthesis of these ideologies involves a commitment to inclusive governance. Decision-making processes should be participatory, drawing on the principles of both ideologies to ensure that the diverse voices of Sudanese citizens are heard. The aim is to create a society where collective welfare and individual freedom coexist harmoniously.

As Sudan endeavors to strike this delicate balance, it must be guided by a commitment to pragmatism and flexibility. The model that emerges should be tailored to Sudanese realities, acknowledging the unique historical context and cultural diversity that define the nation. In this synthesis, Sudan may find a blueprint for a future where the collective aspirations of its people find resonance with the principles of justice, prosperity, and unity.

## Sudan's Unique Path: Why Both Are Necessary

Sudan stands at a crossroads, poised to redefine its narrative through a nuanced integration of both Communism and Capitalism. The necessity for embracing elements from both ideologies lies in the recognition of the nation's unique historical, cultural, and economic context. It is a journey towards a Sudanese model that marries the collective vision of Communism with the economic dynamism of Capitalism.

The historical landscape of Sudan, marked by periods of conflict and fragmentation, necessitates a comprehensive approach that addresses both economic disparities and social divides. Communism offers a lens through which the scars of historical injustices can be healed. By advocating for collective ownership, Sudan can forge a path towards a society that values unity, social justice, and shared prosperity.

Simultaneously, the entrepreneurial spirit embedded in Capitalism can be harnessed to propel Sudan towards economic vitality. A strategic application of free-market principles can stimulate innovation, create job opportunities, and foster a culture of self-reliance. For a nation seeking to ascend from the depths of historical challenges, a balanced infusion of Capitalist dynamism becomes an essential catalyst for progress.

Sudan's unique path lies in the fusion of these seemingly opposing ideologies. It is a recognition that the nation's strengths lie in its diversity, and a one-size-fits-all approach is insufficient. By embracing both Communism and Capitalism, Sudan can fashion a society where the collective spirit is the bedrock of societal well-being, and individual initiative is the driving force behind economic prosperity.

Moreover, the synthesis of these ideologies is not a static concept; it evolves with the changing needs and dynamics of Sudanese society. Flexibility becomes paramount in crafting policies that respond to emerging challenges while staying true to the core values of justice, equality, and economic vibrancy.

This unique path towards synthesis is a commitment to inclusive governance, where citizens actively participate in shaping the nation's destiny. It involves creating mechanisms that ensure the benefits of economic prosperity are shared equitably, and the fruits of collective progress are accessible to all Sudanese citizens.

It is imperative to engage in a robust national discourse. The voices of citizens from diverse backgrounds must contribute to the dialogue, shaping policies that reflect the aspirations of the people. The synthesis of Communism and Capitalism becomes not just a theoretical construct but a living, breathing embodiment of Sudan's determination to forge a future that encapsulates the dreams and visions of its people.

In navigating this intricate path, Sudan has the opportunity to redefine its place on the global stage. By leveraging the strengths of both ideologies, the nation can establish a socio-political framework that is uniquely Sudanese—one that harmonizes collective unity with individual freedom, creating a legacy that resonates through generations.

In the exploration of Communism and Capitalism within the Sudanese context, we unveil a narrative rich with potential, complexity, and the promise of a united nation. As we reflect on the ideologies discussed, it becomes evident that neither Communism nor Capitalism, in isolation, can fully address Sudan's multifaceted challenges. The true essence lies in the delicate fusion of both—a synthesis that embraces the collective vision of Communism and the economic dynamism of Capitalism.

Sudan's historical tapestry, woven with threads of conflict and diversity, calls for a comprehensive approach that speaks to the heart of its societal complexities. Communism, with its emphasis on collective ownership and social justice, becomes a balm for historical wounds, offering a path towards unity and shared prosperity. Simultaneously, the entrepreneurial spirit championed by Capitalism emerges as a dynamic force propelling Sudan towards economic vitality and individual empowerment.

The necessity for balancing these ideologies is not a concession to political compromise but a strategic recognition of Sudan's unique path. It is an acknowledgment that the nation's strengths lie in its diversity, and a holistic approach that integrates both ideologies is essential for sustainable progress.

As Sudan navigates this uncharted territory, the journey towards synthesis is not without its challenges. It demands a commitment to inclusivity, where the voices of all citizens contribute to shaping the nation's destiny. It calls for flexibility, recognizing that the socio-political framework must evolve to address emerging needs and aspirations. Moreover, it is a call to action for robust national discourse, where the dreams and visions of the people are woven into the fabric of Sudanese governance.

This synthesis is not a static destination but a dynamic process—a living embodiment of Sudan's determination to forge a future that encapsulates the dreams and visions of its people. It is an invitation for Sudanese citizens to actively participate in shaping policies that reflect their collective aspirations.

In conclusion, as we envision a Sudan that harmonizes collective unity with individual freedom, we embark on a transformative journey towards a socio-political framework uniquely Sudanese. The synergy between Communism and Capitalism becomes the catalyst for a legacy that resonates through generations—a legacy of a united Sudan, standing tall on the global stage, embodying the dreams and visions that propel it towards a future of prosperity, justice, and unity.

# Chapter 15: Idealisms of Tribalism

In the heart of Sudan, where the sun kisses the vast landscapes and whispers tales of ages past, a mosaic of diverse tribes weaves the intricate tapestry of the nation's identity. As we embark on this exploration of tribalism, envision yourself standing at the crossroads of tradition and evolution, where the echoes of history beckon us to unravel the complexities that define us as Sudanese.

Picture this: a bustling marketplace, alive with the vibrant hues of traditional attire, resonating with the rhythmic beats of indigenous music. Here, amidst the kaleidoscope of faces adorned with cultural pride, tribal affiliations stand as pillars of strength and identity. Yet, beneath the surface, lies a nuanced history that has shaped the dynamics of this beautiful nation.

Sudan, like a phoenix rising from the ashes, has weathered the storms of tribalism—sometimes a source of unity, at other times a turbulent sea threatening to engulf the promise of a united nation. As we traverse the historical pathways of these tribes, let us navigate the ebbs and flows, understanding the dual nature of tribalism that both binds us to our roots and challenges our journey towards a more evolved Sudan.

In the warmth of the Sudanese sun, let us delve into the heart of tribal heritage—a realm where stories are etched in the sands of time, and the legacy of our ancestors intertwines with the present. It is a place where tradition dances with modernity, and the echoes of ancient customs resonate in the contemporary heartbeat of our nation.

But, as the sun casts its long shadows, we must acknowledge that the richness of our tribal diversity has not always been a seamless symphony. It has been, at times, a cacophony of discord, echoing through history with tales of conflict and strife that have tested the resilience of our collective spirit. Tribalism, in its lowest regard, has been a double-edged sword, both a source of cultural pride and a catalyst for internal discord.

Yet, from the shadows emerges a beacon of hope, casting light on the highest regards of tribalism. Within the cultural richness and deep-rooted traditions lies a tapestry of unity waiting to be woven—a tapestry that not only celebrates our differences but also binds us as one Sudanese family.

As we tread the historical footprints of our tribes, let us not only explore the conflicts but also draw inspiration from the triumphs, recognizing that tribal affiliations can be a wellspring of strength and identity. Our heritage, intricately woven with threads of resilience, becomes a bridge between the past and the future—a bridge that we must traverse to reach the destined evolution that beckons Sudan.

So, dear reader, fasten your seatbelt for a journey through time and tradition, as we navigate the contours of tribalism, understanding its lows and highs. As the sun sets on the horizon, let us embark on this exploration with open hearts, for within the folds of tribalism lies the story of Sudan's metamorphosis—a story waiting to be told.

## The Lowliest Regards of Tribalism

Within the intricate tapestry of Sudan's historical legacy, the lowliest regards of tribalism weave a narrative that has left an indelible mark on the collective consciousness of the nation. The roots of tribal divisions delve deep into the annals of time, tracing their origins to a complex interplay of cultural, social, and historical factors.

- Origins of Tribal Divisions:

Explore the historical origins of tribal divisions, dating back to pre-colonial times and the early formations of distinct ethnic identities.

Uncover the impact of external influences, such as colonial rule, in exacerbating tribal differences and creating a legacy that persists to this day.

- Tribal Conflicts in Historical Context:

Examine specific historical instances where tribal conflicts emerged as a significant challenge to the unity of Sudan.

Shed light on how these conflicts were often fueled by external powers seeking to exploit divisions for their own interests.

- Colonial Legacy:

Analyze the role of colonial powers in manipulating tribal identities and creating artificial hierarchies to maintain control.

Discuss how the legacy of colonial-era policies and practices has perpetuated tribal tensions and hindered national cohesion.

- Impact on Cultural Heritage:

Delve into the consequences of tribal conflicts on Sudan's rich cultural heritage.

Highlight instances where the suppression of certain cultural practices or the dominance of one tribe over another has led to a loss of cultural diversity.

- Historical Wounds and Resentments:

Explore the lingering wounds and resentments that have been passed down through generations as a result of historical tribal conflicts.

Discuss how these historical legacies continue to shape perceptions and interactions among different tribes.

In dissecting the historical legacy of tribalism, it becomes evident that the lowliest regards have roots deeply embedded in a complex web of historical events. Understanding this legacy is crucial in unraveling the layers of tribal dynamics and paving the way for a more harmonious and united Sudan. As we confront the echoes of the past, we lay the groundwork for a collective healing that transcends historical divisions and propels us toward a future characterized by unity and resilience.

## Conflict and Strife

In the intricate narrative of Sudan's history, the lowest manifestations of tribalism unravel a tale steeped in conflict and strife. Within the confines of our collective past, tribal affiliations have not always been the threads weaving a harmonious identity; instead, they have, at times, ignited tensions that echo through the annals of time.

As we navigate the historical landscape, instances arise where tribal conflicts have cast shadows over the unity of Sudan. These conflicts, rooted in the diversity of tribal identities, have often become flashpoints, revealing the intricate interplay of geographical, cultural, and political factors. What emerges is a nuanced tapestry of discord, ranging from localized disputes to more widespread confrontations that have left lasting imprints on the national psyche.

These internal skirmishes, fueled by tribal affiliations, carry profound consequences for the stability of Sudan. Communities find themselves caught in the crossfire, with displacement and disruptions becoming the harrowing aftermath. The very essence of daily life is disrupted as tribal conflicts unfold, creating fault lines that challenge the harmonious coexistence our nation aspires to achieve.

In the wake of these conflicts, the shadows of tribal strife linger, casting doubt on the vision of a united Sudan. It becomes imperative to unravel the layers of historical strife and discern the lessons imprinted in the scars of our past. Understanding the roots of conflict and strife is not merely an exercise in historical reflection; it is a crucial step towards healing the wounds that tribal divisions have inflicted upon the collective soul of our nation.

Through the exploration of conflict and strife, we confront the uncomfortable realities that have hindered the progress of Sudan. It is an acknowledgment of the challenges posed by the lowliest regards of tribalism, urging us to seek a future where unity prevails over discord. In navigating these troubled waters, we find the strength to forge a path towards a Sudan that rises above historical tensions, embracing a narrative of resilience and collective growth.

## Stagnation and Isolation

In the shadow of tribalism's lowest facets lies the subtle yet profound impact it exerts on the trajectory of individual and collective growth within Sudan. This examination unveils a narrative where tribal affiliations, rather than acting as catalysts for progress, often become impediments that stagnate the development of both individuals and the nation as a whole.

As we delve into the intricacies of tribalism's hindrance on individual growth, it becomes apparent that the boundaries drawn by tribal affiliations can confine personal aspirations. In a society where tribal identity is accorded significant weight, individuals may find their opportunities limited by the expectations and norms associated with their specific tribe. This stifling environment hampers the natural evolution of talents, ideas, and ambitions, preventing the diverse potential within Sudan's population from fully blossoming.

Furthermore, the impact extends beyond the individual to the collective aspirations of the nation. Excessive tribalism creates a fragmented landscape, hindering the collaborative efforts required for a united and prosperous Sudan. The pooling of resources, skills, and talents across tribal lines is impeded, resulting in a collective potential that remains largely untapped. This stagnation becomes a barrier to the realization of a shared national vision where the strengths of one tribe complement those of another, propelling the entire nation forward.

In addition to hindering growth, excessive tribalism fosters isolationist tendencies that permeate both individual and communal spheres. Communities become insular, interacting primarily within the confines of their tribal boundaries. This isolation hampers the free exchange of ideas, cultural practices, and innovations between tribes, further limiting the potential for cross-pollination of perspectives that could contribute to a richer and more dynamic national identity.

As tribalism fosters isolation, the once vibrant tapestry of Sudan's cultural diversity starts to fray at the edges. The nation risks losing the opportunity to draw upon the wealth of traditions, practices, and knowledge held by each tribe. This isolationist tendency, born out of the excessive emphasis on tribal differences, stands as a roadblock to the collective flourishing that comes from embracing the diversity within Sudan.

In confronting these challenges, it becomes clear that to foster individual and collective growth, Sudan must transcend the limitations imposed by excessive tribalism. Embracing a more inclusive narrative—one that values the contributions of each tribe while fostering unity and collaboration—holds the key to unlocking the true potential of Sudanese individuals and the nation as a whole. Only then can Sudan rise above stagnation and isolation, charting a course toward a future defined by shared growth and prosperity.

## The Highest Regards of Tribalism

In the exploration of tribalism's highest regards, we uncover a narrative that transcends the shadows of discord and strives to illuminate the positive facets of Sudan's rich tapestry of cultures. Far from being solely a source of division, tribal affiliations, when regarded in their highest regard, emerge as pillars supporting the foundation of a united and culturally vibrant nation.

*Celebrating the Cultural Richness:*

At the zenith of tribalism lies the celebration of cultural richness. Each tribe within Sudan contributes a unique thread to the intricate fabric of the nation's identity. From distinct customs and languages to rich folklore and artistic expressions, the highest regards of tribalism emphasize the cultural wealth that each tribe brings to the collective heritage of Sudan. It is a celebration of diversity, a recognition that the nation's strength lies in the mosaic of traditions interwoven into its cultural tapestry.

*Preserving Heritage and Identity:*

Tribal affiliations, when held in high esteem, become custodians of historical continuity. The highest regards of tribalism emphasize the importance of preserving and passing down cultural heritage from one generation to the next. This preservation of identity becomes a powerful force that anchors individuals within a broader historical context, instilling a sense of pride and belonging. Each tribe becomes a living testament to the enduring legacy of Sudanese history.

*Lessons from History:*

Within the highest regards of tribalism lies the wisdom gleaned from the pages of history. Tribes, when celebrated for their positive contributions, become repositories of knowledge, passing down lessons, values, and traditions that have withstood the tests of time. This recognition of the positive historical role played by tribes encourages a harmonious coexistence, where the strengths of one tribe complement those of another, fostering a collective understanding of Sudanese history.

*Unity in Diversity:*

The highest regards of tribalism envision a Sudan where tribal affiliations are not divisive lines but threads that weave together a harmonious unity. It is an understanding that, while tribes may differ in customs, traditions, and languages, they collectively contribute to the greater whole. This unity in diversity becomes a cornerstone for a nation that flourishes on the strength derived from the unique attributes each tribe brings to the table.

As we ascend to the highest regards of tribalism, we find a Sudan that embraces the positive aspects of cultural diversity, cherishes historical continuity, and fosters unity. The vision transcends the boundaries that may have once separated tribes, inviting a collective journey towards a Sudan where tribal affiliations are celebrated as integral components of a thriving national identity. In recognizing the highest regards of tribalism, Sudan charts a course toward a future where the richness of its cultural heritage becomes a unifying force, propelling the nation towards prosperity and resilience.

## The Necessity of Evolution

As we navigate through the intricacies of Sudan's historical tapestry, the imperative of evolution emerges as a guiding beacon—a call to transcend the confines of tribalism and embark on a collective journey toward progress and unity.

*Unity and Progress:*

At the core of the necessity for evolution lies the idea that unity is the linchpin for national progress. Sudan stands at a crossroads where tribal affiliations, once divisive, must evolve into threads weaving a cohesive narrative of unity. A united front becomes the catalyst for collective success, breaking down the barriers that hinder collaboration and hindering the realization of Sudan's full potential.

*Economic Growth:*

The evolution beyond tribal boundaries is not merely a philosophical pursuit but a practical necessity for economic growth. A nation fragmented by tribal divisions is akin to a garden deprived of essential nutrients. To flourish, Sudan must embrace the collaborative efforts of all tribes, pooling resources, skills, and talents. This collaborative approach becomes the cornerstone for economic development, propelling the nation towards prosperity and fostering a future where every tribe contributes to the collective wealth.

*Global Integration:*

The imperative for evolution extends beyond national borders. Sudan, positioned on the global stage, must shed the shackles of excessive tribalism to become an active participant in the international community. A nation that embraces diversity and unity becomes a beacon of cooperation, contributing to global endeavors and redefining its role in the interconnected world. The journey toward global integration becomes a testament to Sudan's evolution and its commitment to fostering diplomatic, economic, and cultural ties on a global scale.

In acknowledging the necessity for evolution, Sudan confronts the reality that the path to progress requires a departure from the historical shackles of tribalism. It is a call to chart a new course, one where the unity of the nation takes precedence over divisive affiliations, and where the collective strength harnessed from diverse tribal contributions propels Sudan to new heights.

The evolution must be comprehensive, transcending not only political and economic realms but also societal and cultural spheres. Sudan's journey toward evolution demands a commitment to fostering an inclusive and tolerant society, where the richness of cultural diversity becomes a source of strength rather than division.

In navigating the necessity of evolution, Sudan lays the groundwork for a future that embraces change, growth, and unity. It is a transformative journey, acknowledging the challenges posed by historical tribal dynamics while steadfastly steering towards a destiny where the nation stands united, resilient, and poised for a prosperous and harmonious future.

## Tribalism as a Historical Relic

As we traverse the historical landscape of Sudan, envisioning a future marked by evolution and unity, the concept of tribalism emerges as a historical relic—an artifact of the past that must be carefully examined, understood, and ultimately consigned to the annals of history. This transition from a present defined by tribal dynamics to a future where tribalism becomes a historical relic is a crucial phase in Sudan's journey towards a more harmonious and united nation.

*Comparisons to Museums:*

In likening tribalism to a historical relic, we draw parallels to museums —a space where artifacts of the past are preserved for reflection, understanding, and education. In this context, tribalism, with its historical roots and implications, becomes a subject for careful examination. By placing it metaphorically within the halls of a museum, Sudan acknowledges the importance of understanding the historical context of tribalism while signaling a departure from its active role in shaping the nation's destiny.

*Preserving Tribal History for Educational Purposes:*

As tribalism transitions into a historical relic, there is a concerted effort to preserve its history for educational purposes. The stories of tribal conflicts, cultural practices, and the impact of tribal affiliations on Sudanese society are not forgotten but rather archived and shared. By preserving this history, Sudan ensures that future generations are equipped with a comprehensive understanding of the nation's complex past, fostering a sense of collective responsibility to steer away from the pitfalls of excessive tribalism.

*The Path to Pluralism:*

Tribalism as a historical relic signifies a pivotal shift towards pluralism—a recognition that diversity can coexist harmoniously within the fabric of Sudanese identity. Pluralism becomes the guiding principle, encouraging the celebration of different tribal traditions, languages, and customs without the baggage of historical animosities. Sudan envisions a future where the relics of tribalism become artifacts of a bygone era, replaced by a pluralistic society that thrives on shared values and mutual respect.

*A Relic of an Important Figure:*

Within the metaphorical museum of Sudan's history, tribalism becomes a relic of an important figure—an embodiment of lessons learned and challenges overcome. It serves as a reminder of the transformative journey the nation has undertaken, where the recognition of tribal affiliations as both a source of pride and a historical challenge paved the way for a united and resilient Sudan. This relic symbolizes the nation's commitment to a future where unity, tolerance, and progress reign supreme.

In navigating the transition of tribalism into a historical relic, Sudan embraces the opportunity to redefine its narrative. By critically examining the historical artifact of tribalism, the nation lays the groundwork for a future where the lessons learned from the past contribute to a more inclusive, tolerant, and united society. It is a forward-looking stance, acknowledging the complexities of history while forging a path towards a Sudan that transcends the shadows of tribalism, standing tall as a symbol of resilience and progress.

As we stand at the culmination of this exploration into the intricate dynamics of tribalism in Sudan, the journey reveals a narrative that traverses the highs and lows, the challenges and triumphs, and ultimately, the transformative potential that lies within the nation's grasp. Sudan's odyssey is one marked by a profound understanding of tribalism—a force that has shaped its history and, in turn, has been shaped by the resilience of its people.

The overarching message emanating from this narrative is one of evolution and unity. The recognition of tribalism's dual nature, with its lows marked by conflicts and divisions and its highs celebrated as a source of cultural richness, lays the foundation for a Sudan that aspires towards collective growth and harmony. It is an acknowledgment that the richness of Sudanese identity lies in the mosaic of tribal affiliations, each contributing to the nation's cultural wealth.

The imperative of evolution stands as a rallying call for Sudan to transcend historical divisions, recognizing that the unity of its people is the linchpin for progress. Evolution requires a departure from the lowliest regards of tribalism, where conflicts have hindered individual and collective growth, to the highest regards, where cultural diversity is celebrated, and tribal affiliations become threads in the tapestry of a united nation.

In envisioning tribalism as a historical relic, Sudan takes a bold step towards a future where the lessons of the past become a guiding light. The metaphorical museum of Sudanese history holds the relics of tribalism as artifacts, inviting reflection, understanding, and a commitment to unity. The recognition of tribal history for educational purposes becomes a testament to Sudan's determination to learn from the past, ensuring that future generations are equipped with the knowledge to navigate the complexities of tribal dynamics.

As we conclude this exploration, Sudan emerges not only as a nation with a complex history but as a beacon of resilience, unity, and the potential for transformative change. The path forward beckons Sudan to embrace pluralism, where the relics of tribalism become symbols of a bygone era. The narrative of Sudan's journey is one of hope—a hope for a future where unity prevails, diversity is celebrated, and the nation stands as a testament to the triumph of collective strength over historical challenges. In closing, Sudan's story is not just a reflection on tribalism; it is a testament to the nation's enduring spirit and its unwavering commitment to a future that transcends the shadows of the past, embracing a destiny defined by unity, prosperity, and resilience.

# Chapter 16: Language

In the tapestry of human history, language weaves the threads of culture, identity, and aspiration. As the poet Rumi once mused, *'The beauty you see in me is a reflection of you.'* Indeed, language is a mirror reflecting the essence of a nation, and in the case of Sudan, it is a mirror that reveals the resilience, aspirations, and dreams of a people. It is a symphony of words that transcends boundaries, shaping the very soul of a nation.

This chapter will serve as a profound impact language holds in the narrative of transformation. It is more than a mere tool of communication; it is the heartbeat of our shared experiences, echoing through the bustling urban landscapes and the serene corners of our villages. Language is the vessel through which dreams are articulated, wisdom is passed down, and unity is forged.

In the context of Sudan's resurgence, language becomes not merely a linguistic instrument but a catalyst for change, a force capable of shaping destinies. As we navigate the intricate terrain of linguistic choices, the underlying current is one of optimism and purpose. Language, in its myriad forms, has the power to redefine our collective narrative. It is an integral part of the symphony we orchestrate as a nation, each dialect contributing a unique note to the melody of Sudanese identity.

In contemplating the future, we envision a linguistic landscape where the richness of our heritage is preserved, and the doors to global opportunities swing wide open. The choice of languages becomes not just a matter of communication but a strategic decision influencing education, innovation, and the very fabric of our society.

Join me in this exploration of language—a journey that transcends mere words and ushers us into a realm where the linguistic tapestry of Sudan is carefully woven, reflecting the dreams and visions that illuminate our path to a brighter tomorrow.

## The Power of Language

Exploring the profound impact of language reveals it as a potent force that extends far beyond the realm of mere communication. Language is the silent architect shaping the thoughts, beliefs, and values of a society. It serves as a vehicle for cultural expression, encapsulating the collective consciousness of a nation. In Sudan's narrative of transformation, language emerges as a powerful tool, capable of instigating positive change and steering the course of progress.

Consider the transformative potential of language within the context of Sudan's journey. As we communicate with one another, we are not merely exchanging words but fostering a shared understanding that lays the foundation for societal growth. The language we use becomes the medium through which ideas are disseminated, innovations are conceptualized, and national unity is cultivated.

Language is a conduit for the dreams and aspirations of a nation. Through the carefully chosen words and expressions, we articulate a vision that transcends the present, envisioning a Sudan that is united, prosperous, and globally connected. In the symphony of Sudanese identity, language plays a crucial role in composing the notes of hope, resilience, and determination.

As we reflect on the power of language, it becomes evident that our linguistic choices are not arbitrary but strategic. The words we use shape our educational landscape, influencing how knowledge is disseminated and acquired. The language we adopt is a key determinant of our ability to participate in the global exchange of ideas, opening doors to economic opportunities and technological advancements.

In Sudan's journey of resurgence, language stands as a silent ally, steering the collective consciousness toward a future defined by progress and unity. It is not merely a means of expression; it is a force that propels us forward, shaping the very fabric of our society. As we navigate the linguistic landscape, let us recognize the transformative power embedded in the words we choose, for it is through language that the dreams and visions of a united Sudan find resonance and take root.

## English as the Primary Language

The decision to establish English as the primary language in Sudan is rooted in a strategic vision for the nation's future. Recognizing the globalized landscape of the 21st century, where communication transcends borders, English emerges as a unifying force. It is a language that connects nations, facilitates international collaboration, and provides access to a vast repository of knowledge.

English, as the primary language, becomes more than a means of communication; it is a gateway to global opportunities. By adopting English as the cornerstone of educational curriculum and official communication, Sudan positions itself on the international stage, fostering a linguistic environment that aligns with the demands of a rapidly evolving world.

The role of English in promoting education and innovation cannot be overstated. It becomes the language of science, technology, and progress, ensuring that Sudanese citizens are equipped with the skills and knowledge needed to navigate the complexities of the modern era. English proficiency opens doors to academic exchanges, research collaborations, and economic ventures, positioning Sudan as an active participant in the global community.

While the adoption of English as the primary language is a forward-looking choice, it also acknowledges the historical context of Sudan. It reflects an openness to embrace linguistic diversity and harness the strengths of multiple languages. The coexistence of English with other languages, such as Arabic and tribal languages, creates a harmonious linguistic tapestry that celebrates Sudan's rich heritage while propelling it towards a future of global significance.

However, it is essential to address potential concerns and challenges associated with this linguistic shift. Ensuring equitable access to English education, preserving the cultural nuances embedded in native languages, and fostering a sense of inclusivity are integral aspects of successfully implementing English as the primary language. The decision is not about diminishing the value of other languages but about strategically positioning Sudan to thrive in an interconnected world, where linguistic adaptability is a key to success.

## Arabic as the Second Language

In crafting a linguistic framework for Sudan's future, the decision to designate Arabic as the second language is both strategic and reflective of historical and cultural ties. Arabic holds a special place in Sudanese identity, representing a connection to the region and a rich heritage that spans centuries.

Recognizing the prevalence of Arabic as a regional and international language, its inclusion as the second language serves as a bridge between Sudan and neighboring nations. This linguistic choice acknowledges the importance of maintaining strong ties with Arab-speaking countries, fostering diplomatic relations, and facilitating cultural exchanges.

Arabic becomes a key asset in regional and international communication, offering Sudanese citizens the ability to engage in dialogue with a broader audience. As a language deeply embedded in the historical and religious fabric of Sudan, it stands as a testament to the nation's heritage and a means to preserve cultural nuances that have shaped the identity of its people.

The strategic positioning of Arabic as the second language is not a negation of the prominence of English. Instead, it complements the global focus of English with a regional perspective, ensuring that Sudan remains well-connected within the Arab world. This linguistic duality allows for a more nuanced and inclusive approach to communication, catering to diverse audiences both at home and abroad.

By embracing Arabic as the second language, Sudan affirms its commitment to a harmonious coexistence of linguistic diversity. The vision is not one of dominance but of balance, recognizing the multifaceted identity of Sudanese society. In this linguistic landscape, Arabic emerges as a bridge that spans not only across nations but also across time, connecting the modern Sudanese identity with the historical roots that define it.

## Preserving Tribal Languages

As we delve deeper into Sudan's linguistic evolution, an integral aspect emerges — the preservation of tribal languages. These languages, deeply rooted in the cultural tapestry of Sudan, carry the stories, traditions, and unique identities of various communities. Acknowledging and safeguarding these tribal languages is an essential commitment to the preservation of the nation's rich heritage.

Tribal languages, spoken in smaller communities, become the carriers of local wisdom and historical narratives. They are the threads that weave the intricate patterns of Sudanese diversity, contributing to the vibrant mosaic of the nation. The decision to preserve tribal languages is a recognition of the intrinsic value embedded in each dialect, fostering a sense of belonging and identity among diverse communities.

In smaller towns and villages, where the intimate fabric of community life is woven through shared stories and local traditions, tribal languages play a pivotal role. These languages are the conduits through which knowledge is passed down from generation to generation, ensuring that the collective memory of Sudanese communities remains intact.

Preserving tribal languages is not just an act of cultural conservation; it is a commitment to inclusivity. It acknowledges the rights of smaller communities to express themselves in their native tongues, fostering a sense of pride and continuity. In doing so, Sudan embraces linguistic diversity not as a challenge but as an asset, enriching the broader narrative of the nation.

This commitment extends beyond mere rhetoric to practical measures. Initiatives that support the teaching and learning of tribal languages, particularly in local schools and community centers, become integral to the preservation effort. By integrating these languages into educational curricula, Sudan ensures that future generations inherit not only the linguistic richness of their communities but also a profound connection to their roots.

In essence, the preservation of tribal languages becomes a pledge to uphold the holistic identity of Sudan. It is a testament to the nation's commitment to honor its past while forging ahead into a future that cherishes the diversity that defines its people. The linguistic landscape, thus adorned with the myriad hues of tribal languages, becomes a true reflection of Sudan's commitment to unity in diversity.

## Latuka and Other Tribal Languages

Within the spectrum of tribal languages, Latuka emerges as a significant thread in Sudan's linguistic tapestry. As we delve into the narrative of Latuka and other tribal languages, we uncover the unique characteristics and contributions that distinguish them within the broader context of Sudanese culture.

Latuka, spoken by a distinct community, becomes a symbol of the intricate cultural diversity that defines Sudan. Its unique linguistic nuances carry the essence of a specific group's history, traditions, and worldview. By acknowledging the importance of Latuka and other tribal languages, Sudan celebrates the distinctiveness embedded in each community's mode of expression.

In recognizing Latuka, we go beyond the linguistic aspects; we appreciate the cultural richness it encapsulates. Tribal languages like Latuka are not merely vehicles of communication; they serve as vessels for preserving customs, folklore, and the collective memory of a people. The decision to honor and protect these languages is a commitment to the preservation of unique identities within Sudan's mosaic.

Moreover, the celebration of Latuka and other tribal languages is an acknowledgment of the intelligence and creativity inherent in each linguistic tradition. These languages are not barriers; they are bridges connecting individuals within their communities. They serve as the lifeblood of smaller societies, fostering a sense of unity and shared identity that transcends words alone.

While English and Arabic may serve as bridges to the global and regional spheres, Latuka and other tribal languages become bridges within local communities. They are the threads that bind neighbors, friends, and families, creating a sense of belonging that is deeply rooted in the linguistic landscape of Sudan.

In the broader context, the celebration of Latuka and other tribal languages underscores Sudan's commitment to preserving its cultural heritage. It is an affirmation that linguistic diversity is not a challenge but a source of strength. By valuing and nurturing these languages, Sudan takes a step towards building a society where every voice is heard, every identity is acknowledged, and every linguistic tradition contributes to the harmonious melody of the nation.

## Language Education Initiatives

The vision for Sudan's linguistic landscape extends beyond mere coexistence to active initiatives that promote multilingual education. Language education becomes a cornerstone in the pursuit of unity, understanding, and shared progress. Initiatives designed to foster linguistic diversity within educational frameworks are instrumental in shaping a society that values the richness of its linguistic tapestry.

In implementing language education initiatives, the focus is not solely on English or Arabic but on embracing the multitude of languages that contribute to Sudan's cultural mosaic. The curriculum is designed to reflect the linguistic diversity of the nation, ensuring that students are exposed to the nuances of English, Arabic, and tribal languages. By doing so, Sudan aims to cultivate a generation that is not only proficient in multiple languages but also appreciates the unique beauty each language brings to the nation's identity.

Language programs extend beyond the walls of traditional classrooms to encompass community-based learning initiatives. Local schools and community centers become hubs where the younger generation is immersed in the cultural richness of tribal languages. This approach serves a dual purpose – it preserves linguistic heritage while nurturing a sense of pride and identity among students.

Recognizing the importance of early language acquisition, Sudan invests in comprehensive language education from primary levels. English and Arabic, being global and regional languages, receive particular emphasis, ensuring that students are well-equipped for national and international engagement. At the same time, tribal languages are integrated into the curriculum, fostering an environment where linguistic diversity is celebrated from the outset of a child's educational journey.

Beyond the curriculum, language education initiatives also focus on teacher training. Educators are provided with resources and professional development opportunities that enable them to effectively teach and appreciate the diverse linguistic backgrounds of their students. In doing so, Sudan ensures that language education becomes a holistic and inclusive experience, reinforcing the importance of linguistic diversity at every level of the education system.

These initiatives go hand in hand with broader efforts to promote literacy in all languages, providing individuals with the tools to engage in the global exchange of ideas. By investing in language education, Sudan not only cultivates linguistic proficiency but also lays the foundation for a society that cherishes its diverse linguistic heritage, fostering unity and understanding among its people.

## Overcoming Linguistic Barriers

As Sudan embarks on the path of embracing linguistic diversity, it becomes imperative to address potential challenges associated with the adoption of a multilingual approach. Overcoming linguistic barriers is not merely a practical consideration but a strategic imperative for creating a harmonious and inclusive society where every citizen feels valued and heard.

One challenge lies in ensuring equitable access to English education, particularly in regions where resources may be limited. Recognizing this, Sudan implements targeted initiatives to bridge the educational gap, ensuring that students across the nation, regardless of geographic location, have access to quality English language instruction. This inclusivity extends to Arabic and tribal languages, where efforts are made to provide equal educational opportunities for all.

Preserving the cultural nuances embedded in native languages is another aspect of overcoming linguistic barriers. Sudan acknowledges that language is not just a means of communication but a carrier of cultural identity. Initiatives are launched to document and celebrate linguistic diversity, ensuring that the essence of each language is preserved and passed down through generations.

A significant consideration is fostering a sense of inclusivity within a multilingual framework. Sudan recognizes that a diverse linguistic landscape can sometimes lead to feelings of exclusion. In response, community-based programs are initiated to promote linguistic exchange and understanding. These programs encourage open dialogue, creating spaces where individuals from different linguistic backgrounds can share their experiences, fostering a sense of belonging and mutual respect.

Practical solutions are devised to facilitate communication across languages. Translation services, language interpretation programs, and other tools are implemented to bridge language gaps in various settings, from governmental institutions to community gatherings. By investing in these practical solutions, Sudan ensures that linguistic diversity does not become a barrier to effective communication and collaboration.

At the heart of overcoming linguistic barriers is a mindset shift. Sudan endeavors to cultivate a national consciousness that values and celebrates linguistic diversity as an asset rather than a challenge. Public awareness campaigns emphasize the importance of linguistic inclusivity, encouraging citizens to embrace the beauty and richness that each language brings to the national identity.

In addressing linguistic barriers, Sudan not only ensures effective communication but also establishes a foundation for a society where every citizen, regardless of their linguistic background, plays an integral role in the nation's progress. Through thoughtful initiatives and a commitment to inclusivity, Sudan paves the way for a future where linguistic diversity is a source of strength rather than division.

## Language and National Identity

The relationship between language and the shaping of national identity is a nuanced interplay that defines the soul of a nation. In Sudan's context, the linguistic choices made are not merely about communication; they are about crafting a collective identity that encompasses the diverse cultural threads woven into the fabric of the nation.

Language becomes the vehicle through which Sudanese citizens express their shared values, aspirations, and collective memory. The decision to adopt English as the primary language, Arabic as the second language, and preserve tribal languages is a deliberate effort to create a national identity that is inclusive and reflective of Sudan's historical and cultural tapestry.

In this linguistic landscape, English emerges as a symbol of Sudan's aspirations for global connectivity and progress. It represents an open door to the world, inviting international collaboration, fostering economic opportunities, and positioning Sudan as an active participant in the global community. Arabic, on the other hand, ties Sudan to its regional roots, reinforcing connections with neighboring Arab-speaking nations and celebrating the historical ties that bind the region together.

The preservation of tribal languages is a commitment to acknowledging the unique identities within Sudan. It signifies a dedication to inclusivity, ensuring that the distinct voices of various communities are not only heard but celebrated. These tribal languages contribute to the mosaic of Sudanese identity, fostering a sense of unity in diversity that defines the nation.

The linguistic choices made are not about erasing differences but about creating a harmonious melody where each note contributes to the symphony of Sudanese identity. Language, in this context, becomes a unifying force, weaving together the diverse strands of the nation into a tapestry that reflects the resilience, diversity, and aspirations of the Sudanese people.

The vision for language and national identity is not static but dynamic, evolving with the changing dynamics of Sudanese society. It is a continuous dialogue that recognizes the importance of adaptability and inclusivity. Sudan seeks to create a national identity that is resilient in the face of change, one that embraces linguistic diversity as a source of strength and unity.

In essence, language becomes the mirror reflecting the collective consciousness of Sudan. Through deliberate linguistic choices, the nation crafts an identity that honors its past, navigates the present, and envisions a future where every citizen sees themselves as an integral part of the unfolding narrative of Sudanese identity.

As we conclude our exploration of Sudan's linguistic journey, we find ourselves at the crossroads of tradition and progress, diversity and unity. The vision for language in Sudan goes beyond the mere mechanics of communication; it is a profound commitment to crafting a national identity that resonates with the heartbeat of its people.

Through the deliberate choice of English as the primary language, Sudan positions itself on the global stage, embracing the opportunities that come with international connectivity. This choice reflects a forward-looking vision that sees beyond borders, fostering an environment where Sudanese citizens can engage with the world, contribute to global conversations, and partake in the collective progress of humanity.

Arabic, as the second language, becomes a bridge that connects Sudan not only to its regional neighbors but also to its historical roots. It is a recognition of the shared heritage that binds Sudan to the Arab-speaking world, fostering diplomatic ties, cultural exchanges, and reinforcing the nation's place within the broader Arab community.

The preservation of tribal languages stands as a testament to Sudan's commitment to inclusivity and the celebration of its diverse cultural heritage. Each tribal language is a unique expression of identity, a cultural gem that contributes to the rich mosaic of Sudanese society. By preserving these languages, Sudan ensures that the nation's roots remain firmly grounded in the distinct traditions and narratives of its various communities.

In the journey towards a multilingual education system, Sudan invests not only in language proficiency but also in fostering a deep appreciation for linguistic diversity. Language education initiatives become the cornerstone for cultivating a generation that is not only proficient in English, Arabic, and tribal languages but also possesses a profound understanding of the cultural nuances embedded in each.

Overcoming linguistic barriers is a practical necessity, addressed through equitable access to education, community-based programs, and a commitment to fostering inclusivity. Sudan recognizes that linguistic diversity, when navigated thoughtfully, becomes a source of strength, enabling effective communication and collaboration across communities and regions.

In the broader context of national identity, language emerges as a powerful tool for crafting a narrative that encompasses the resilience, aspirations, and unity of the Sudanese people. The linguistic choices made reflect a conscious effort to weave together the diverse threads of Sudanese identity into a tapestry that is both inclusive and dynamic.

As Sudan moves forward, embracing linguistic diversity is not just a strategic decision but a profound acknowledgment of the nation's strength. The linguistic landscape becomes a living testament to Sudan's commitment to unity in diversity, a celebration of the multitude of voices that contribute to the harmonious melody of the nation.

In this concluding chapter, we find Sudan poised at the cusp of a future where linguistic choices serve as a compass, guiding the nation towards prosperity, unity, and a collective identity that is both deeply rooted and ever-evolving. The linguistic journey is a continuous narrative, a story of resilience, progress, and the unwavering spirit of the Sudanese people.

# Conclusion

Ever since my youth, I have carried within me the fervent belief that we, the people of South Sudan and Sudan, are bound together by a shared identity, a unity that transcends any divisions or challenges we may face. This unity, ingrained in our history and cultural heritage, forms the very fabric of our existence. It is the foundation upon which we can build a prosperous and harmonious future. In the complex tapestry of our nations, the threads of unity weave through every chapter of our collective story.

In the journey towards realizing our dreams and visions, it is imperative that we recognize ourselves as one nation, one people. Our destinies are intertwined, and our strength lies in our ability to stand together, resilient against the storms that may come our way. The mirage of greatness for South Sudan and Sudan can only materialize when we acknowledge the power of unity, understanding that despite our differences, we are fundamentally connected. As we strive for a brighter future, let us cultivate a sense of togetherness that will serve as a guiding light through the challenges and triumphs that lie ahead.

The dreams and visions I hold for the Humanity of Sudan (Ofiyok) extend beyond the realms of imagination. Yet, to bring these aspirations to life, there is an urgent call that resonates from the depths of my heart – a call for our dispersed citizens to return home. The echoes of displacement cast shadows on the potential progress of our great nation, and it is time for us to heed the call, to gather our strength and return to the land that cradles our shared history.

The impact of diaspora on our national fabric cannot be underestimated. Our strength lies in our unity, and a scattered population weakens the very foundation upon which our dreams rest. There is a sense of pride and honor that awaits us when we return home, becoming the builders of a united nation. It is in our return that we find the key to evolutionary progress, for a nation cannot thrive when its citizens are scattered, devoid of a collective purpose.

Let us unite in our commitment to building a homeland where pride, honor, and progress intertwine. The call to return home is not just a directive but a summons to be the architects of our destiny, paving the way for younger generations to follow. In our collective return, we fortify the staircase to greater cultural, and heritage linkage, ensuring that our nation stands tall, with a foundation rooted firmly in the soil of our shared identity.

The concept of evolutionary progress is the driving force behind my dreams for the Humanity of Sudan (Ofiyok). It is a vision that transcends mere development – it is a call to embrace a continuous, upward trajectory that propels our nation to new heights. In this vision, the younger generations stand as the builders, crafting a staircase that connects our past to our future, fostering a cultural and heritage linkage that forms the very essence of our identity.

As we embark on this journey of evolutionary progress, we must recognize the pivotal role of the youth. They are not just the future; they are the architects of the present, laying the groundwork for a Sudan that stands as a testament to its rich cultural tapestry. In nurturing the dreams and aspirations of the younger generations, we ensure that our progress is not just sustained but elevated to extraordinary heights.

The economic landscape of a nation is intricately tied to the well-being of its people. In the context of the Humanity of Sudan (Ofiyok), the scattered population poses a significant challenge to economic development. To truly realize our dreams of prosperity, we must understand the economic repercussions of a disunited citizenry and act with a sense of urgency to contribute to the economic growth of our homeland.

Imagine a Sudan where each citizen plays a part in building the economic foundation. The return of the diaspora, bringing back knowledge and skills gained from abroad, becomes a catalyst for economic progress. Our nation's economy, like a delicate ecosystem, requires the active participation of every individual to thrive. As we contribute to economic development, we not only fortify the financial infrastructure but also secure the prosperity of future generations. The call to return home is not merely a call for unity; it is a call for economic empowerment that will elevate Sudan to new heights on the global stage.

In envisioning the transformative journey of the Humanity of Sudan (Ofiyok), political progress emerges as the fundamental building block. Analogous to constructing a sturdy hut, the political framework forms the foundation upon which our national structure stands. It is essential to recognize the dynamic role that both the younger and older generations play in shaping the political landscape of our nation.

The younger generations, armed with the knowledge gained from their adopted countries, become the architects of political growth. As they take the reins, guided by the wisdom of their predecessors, the hut of political progress takes shape. The collaborative effort between generations is crucial, ensuring that the political structure not only stands tall but continues to evolve, adapting to the changing needs of our society. This foundation, when solidified, becomes the stronghold from which we can collectively reach new heights.

The amalgamation of knowledge gleaned from our adopted countries with the wisdom embedded in our roots serves as a powerful catalyst for progress. This fusion of learning, as envisaged for the Humanity of Sudan (Ofiyok), creates a synergy that propels our nation forward. It is not just about returning home; it is about bringing back the wealth of experiences, skills, and innovations acquired abroad to enrich our homeland.

The bridge between the learning of adopted countries and the traditions of our original land becomes a vital conduit for progress. As we embrace our unique intelligence and cultural differences, a wonderful centerpiece takes form – the circle of life for the Humanity of Sudan. This circle is marked by shared attributes, common goals, and a harmonious coexistence that defines the essence of our nation. By congregating not just in geographical locations but in our hearts and minds, we enable our spirits to be the driving force behind mutual agreements and the forward march of Humanity.

The vision for the Humanity of Sudan (Ofiyok) extends beyond the physical structures to the broader infrastructure of our nation. Envision a Sudan where the foundations are broad-based, supported by the collective efforts of its citizens. The imagery is not just of towering buildings but also of deeply rooted grassroots that hold steadfast, ensuring a wider influence that reaches every corner of our land.

As we build this infrastructure, we are not merely constructing physical structures but strengthening the very roots of our society. The interplay between the macro-level developments and the grassroots influence is symbiotic, creating a nation that is remarkably influential and, in many ways, an anomaly. Our progress is not isolated but interconnected, with each citizen contributing to the grand tapestry that represents the evolutionary journey of the Humanity of Sudan (Ofiyok). In embracing this vision, we set the stage for a future where our nation stands as a testament to resilience, unity, and unparalleled progress.

In the culmination of our dreams and visions for the Humanity of Sudan (Ofiyok), there exists an unwavering hope for a nation that transcends the ordinary and stands as a beacon of influence. It is a hope deeply rooted in the collective efforts, resilience, and unity of our people. As we look towards the future, envision a Sudan that not only survives but thrives, becoming an anomaly in the global landscape.

This hope is not just wishful thinking; it is a belief in the potential of our nation to rise above challenges and become a force to be reckoned with. It is a confidence in the abilities of the Sudanese people to shape a brighter future, guided by principles of unity, perseverance, and dedication. The dreams we hold dear are not individual aspirations but a shared vision for a Sudan that is not only remarkably influential but also a source of inspiration for the entire world.

As we move forward, let our collective hope be the driving force that propels us towards a future where the Humanity of Sudan (Ofiyok) shines brightly on the global stage, a testament to the indomitable spirit and limitless potential of our nation.

www.ingramcontent.com/pod-product-compliance
Lightning Source LLC
Chambersburg PA
CBHW060047230426
43661CB00004B/694